MAKING A
SPIRITUAL
WARRIOR

TRINKLE

Colonel Evan J. Trinkle
USA Retired

Confront the Enemy
&
Live in Victory as a Man
After God's Heart

Making a Spiritual Warrior
Confront the Enemy and Live in Victory as a Man After God's Heart

COPYRIGHT © 2015
BY EVAN TRINKLE

First Printing, 2016
Second Printing, 2017

Scripture references used in this book noted (AMP) are taken from the Holy Bible, Amplified Bible, Copyright © 2015 by The Lockman Foundation, La Habra, CA 90631. All rights reserved.

Scripture references used in this book noted (ESV) are taken from the Holy Bible, English Standard Version, Copyright © 2001 by Crossway Bibles, a publishing ministry of Good News Publishers.

Scripture references used in this book noted (HCSB) are taken from the Holy Bible, Holman Christian Standard Bible, Copyright © 1999, 2000, 2002, 2003, 2009 by Holman Bible Publishers, Nashville Tennessee. All rights reserved.

Scripture references used in this book noted (KJV) are taken from the Holy Bible, King James Version, public domain.

Scripture references used in this book noted (MEV) are taken from the Holy Bible, Modern English Version. Copyright © 2014 by Military Bible Association. Published and distributed by Charisma House.

Scripture references used in this book noted (NASB) are taken from the Holy Bible, New American Standard Bible, Copyright © 1960, 1962, 1963, 1968, 1971, 1972, 1973, 1975, 1977, 1995 by The Lockman Foundation.

Scripture references used in this book noted (NET) are taken from the Holy Bible, New English Translation (NET). NET Bible® copyright ©1996-2006 by Biblical Studies Press, L.L.C. http://netbible.com. All rights reserved.

Scripture references used in this book noted (NKJV) are taken from the Holy Bible, New King James Version Copyright © 1982 by Thomas Nelson. Used by permission. All rights reserved.

Scripture references used in this book noted (NIV) are taken from the Holy Bible, New International Version®, NIV® Copyright ©1973, 1978, 1984, 2011 by Biblica, Inc.® Used by permission. All rights reserved worldwide.

Scripture references used in this book noted (TLB) are taken from The Living Bible, copyright © 1971 by Tyndale House Foundation. Used by permission of Tyndale House Publishers Inc., Carol Stream, Illinois. All rights reserved.

Scripture references used in this book noted (YLT) are taken from the Holy Bible, Young's Literal Translation, public domain.

TEXT DESIGN: Arrow Computer Services

Printed in the United States of America

A Very Special Thanks to Steve Gehring

STEVE GEHRING, A NATIVE of Wilmington, Delaware, graduated from Asbury University in 1964. He later attended Asbury Theological Seminary and Wesley Theological Seminary in Washington, D.C., after which he pastored six different Methodist churches on the eastern shore of Maryland. After earning a Master of Arts in Special Education, he served as principal of Lighthouse Christian Academy from 1976 until 1982. In 1983, he was appointed family life and Christian education pastor at First Assembly of God in Lexington, Kentucky. He also served as administrator of Assembly Christian School (now Summit Academy) and had oversight of the adult ministries. He remained as the adult ministries and pastoral care pastor at First Assembly of God until his retirement from the church in 2013. His duties at First Assembly included counseling, teaching adult classes, administering men's ministries, and overseeing the senior adult ministries.

Steve and his wife, Suzanne, reside in Wilmore, Kentucky. Suzanne is the University Archivist at Asbury University. They are the proud parents of four children: Stephanie, Jeff, Andrew, and Tim. They have two grandsons, Jacob and Mason.

Steve is a board-certified pastoral counselor who sees his calling as ministering to men as he imparts the Word of God through retreats and Bible study classes.

Steve's mentorship and guidance during the writing of *Making a Spiritual Warrior* was invaluable. Each lesson was reviewed, and if necessary, comments were provided. Steve's heart for men's ministries is felt as soon as one comes into his presence. His life daily lived out before others reflects the heart of a man's love toward his family and others. I am very thankful for Steve's involvement in "The Warrior Project: the Making of a Warrior" as the theme of this study. Thank you, Steve.

About the Author

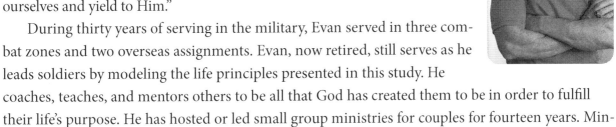

EVAN TRINKLE, A NATIVE of Cortland, New York, has been a Christian since 1978. Through those many years, the Lord has taught Evan many significant life lessons that he would like to share with other men in order to help them navigate the many daily challenges that most men face. The most central lesson is "Life is all about the Lord Jesus Christ and what He has done for us, and what He can do through us, if we will humble ourselves and yield to Him."

During thirty years of serving in the military, Evan served in three combat zones and two overseas assignments. Evan, now retired, still serves as he leads soldiers by modeling the life principles presented in this study. He coaches, teaches, and mentors others to be all that God has created them to be in order to fulfill their life's purpose. He has hosted or led small group ministries for couples for fourteen years. Ministering to families, as well as individuals, is his passion.

Evan graduated from the University of Kentucky in 1984 and met his wife, Ardis, at Asbury College in Wilmore, Kentucky. They reside in Lexington, Kentucky, and have been married since 1982. They have two adult children, Hannah and Elizabeth, and five grandchildren.

Table of Contents

A Letter
From Author Evan Trinkle

"The LORD is a warrior..."
Exodus 15:3 (NET)

THE FIRST EIGHTEEN YEARS of my life were spent without direction from God. I was not reared in the church; in fact, I went only when visiting my grandfather, who was a pastor, or when visiting my friend who had no choice about attending church. I was neither agnostic nor atheist; I just did not have a position or any thoughts about God because I never knew there was a need. I lived my life within the boundaries set before me. I am not going to disclose how sinful my life was. Suffice it to say, I lived my life without being obedient to God, but as I approached my eighteenth birthday, I started to change. I realized there was a void in my life (something was missing; something was not right).

On my nineteenth birthday, I surrendered and dedicated my life to the call God had on it. I was not in a church, but was in my bedroom in my mother's house when I asked God to change my life. Mine was a simple prayer. I said, "God, if You are real, I want to give You a try." I had no direction, only trust and faith that God was going to be faithful to help me and guide my life. My family thought I was a little crazy; my friends scattered as far from me as they could distance themselves. My life changed drastically, but for the first time in my life, I did not feel a void or emptiness. There was peace where there once had been anger, frustration, and restlessness. Even though I did not know where my life was going at the time, there was a confidence in my life that God's grace and mercy would help me. The Holy Spirit of God spoke to me when I read the Bible or listened to other Christians. There was daily a hunger in my life for change. The choice to surrender to God's plan and purpose transformed my life.

I have walked with God now since 1978, and my desire is to be an encouragement and an example to demonstrate hope that God can change your life. Your life doesn't have to be where it is now. *"As iron sharpens iron, so one man sharpens another"* (Proverbs 27:17, NIV). You can be different, and change will come to you daily as you make choices that will result in a different life. Remember, you are not alone; many are experiencing the same struggles you face. I have been through many life-changing circumstances, and in every one of them, God has been faithful to provide me with a Scripture verse from the Bible or a fellow Christian to give a word of advice or encouragement. Sometimes that fellow believer just stood next to me, inspiring me to remain hopeful, persistent, and steadfast.

Abraham was a man like many of us—living his life, living in his community, growing with his relatives, worshipping the familiar gods of those around him. However, Abraham's life changed one day when God called him to be different. He was called to take a bold step. He was called to step away from all that was comfortable to his way of life. His family and relatives questioned his sanity. He had to turn from worshipping the gods of his culture to worshipping the one true God. Abraham left his community for what God was leading him to and daily developed faith and trust in God to walk out this new calling placed on his life.

Abraham had to trust God for many years before he saw the results of his faith and trust in God. His joy came to him because God was faithful to Abraham. God's mercy and promises are for all those who place their lives in His hands.

As I have grown over the years as a man seeking the heart of God, I have learned many life lessons. My desire is that this study will touch your heart and cause you to make a deeper commitment to walk daily with God and that you will have a stronger confidence in God. He wants to have fellowship with us, and He wants us to be men who make and keep the covenant with Him.

Let us all walk together.

Through Christ,

Evan

Endorsements

MY DEAR BROTHER IN Christ, I congratulate you! You are about to embark on a journey of life-changing proportions. This Bible study will deepen your understanding of God's Word and its life-enhancing and life-changing truth.

The Christian life is a journey. Most of the time a journey is completed in stages. Stages indicate that there is a process involved in reaching the destination. In the Christian life, the destination is holiness of life. God uses His divine process to bring us to holiness. This process involves His methods that will take us step by step to where He accomplishes His purpose for our life. Jeremiah 29:11 says, *"I [God] have a plan [process and purpose] for you and it is a good plan—a plan to prosper you."*

Like any journey one decides to take, there is anticipation or dread. The journey can be delightful or a drudgery. Your attitude in this study will determine its impact upon your life. My prayer is that as you engage in this study of God's Word, you will recognize it as one aspect or event of God's divine process to lead you toward a life of holiness. If you will allow God to work in your life, He can and will use this study to move you closer to knowing Him more intimately.

So, my brother, I encourage you to anticipate and enjoy God's revelation for your life.

– Steve Gehring

I HAD THE PRIVILEGE of meeting Evan during an overseas deployment in 2013. During that deployment, he introduced me to a draft of *Making a Spiritual Warrior: Confront the Enemy and Live in Victory as a Man After God's Heart* Bible study. After reading through the study and spending several hours discussing multiple draft iterations, I knew Evan had something special in the making. You will find this study is not your ordinary men's Bible study. If you are ready to take a life-changing journey to truly becoming a man after God's own heart, commit to this study with a group of men and be prepared to have your life transformed. I think you will find the true uniqueness of this Bible study is the Warrior Ring. After completing this study, your transformational covenant is symbolized visually everyday by wearing an attractively designed ring. Wearing the ring is not only a reminder of the covenant you made during the study; it is also a visual expression of your faith. I challenge you to use this visual expression of your faith as an opportunity to share your faith with others verbally. May God bless each of you and your journey to becoming warriors after God's own heart!

– CH (CPT) Mark Hart, MOARNG

ONE OF THE MOST powerful moments I have ever experienced was when I was watching the movie *Saving Private Ryan*. Private Ryan, as an old man, had gone to Arlington National Cemetery to visit the grave of the captain who had given his life to save his. As he is standing there thinking about what the captain had said, he turned to his wife and said, "Tell me I've lived a good life…tell me I'm a good man." It was extremely important to Ryan that he had earned the right to be saved through the sacrifices of all of those men. He wanted to know that he had done well.

Only one thing matters in this life when we get to the end. Not how much money we made. Not how important we became or how much stuff we acquired. We want to know that we did well and that when we look into our Savior's eyes, He will say, "Well done, My good and faithful servant." Evan Trinkle states in his introduction, "Every man's life consists of a journey that will present many crossroads, options, and choices…..often they become defining moments in our life that take us down a road we never intended to travel."

The one thing that I know for certain through the thirty plus years of being a believer is that nothing just happens to us in this life. If we are to overcome and experience the kind of life we can be proud of, it won't be an accident. We must be intentional in our actions and choices to bring about the desired results. A famous person once said, "Carefully watch your thoughts, for they shall become your words. Manage and watch your words, for they shall become your actions. Consider and judge your actions, for they shall become your habits. Acknowledge and watch your habits, for they shall become your values. Understand and embrace your values, for they become your destiny."

Most people allow life to live them and hope for a good outcome. This study has all the basics needed to build our lives on a firm foundation and gives us the tools needed to walk out a life that is pleasing to God. This will enable us to finish well! This study is built upon the understanding of covenant and shows us that every aspect of our life needs to take place within the context of covenant: our covenant with God, with our families, with one another, and with ourselves. I strongly recommend this study for anyone who wants a well-rounded approach to accomplishing a life that is worthy of our high calling in Christ Jesus.

– Michael Hoke, Refreshing Ministries International, Inc.

TO THE READER AND student of *Making a Spiritual Warrior: Confront the Enemy and Live in Victory as a Man After God's Heart*, I would like to provide you with my strongest endorsement of this study. I think you'll find, as I did, that you will be challenged as you progress through these lessons. During this study, you will have to look inward and examine your relationship not only with God but also with your family and those you call friends. I know you will find, as you participate with your group, that the author has provided you with the biblical tools to become the strongest warrior and man after God's own heart you possibly can be. I was personally challenged by the study to take a hard look at my relationship with the Lord. By answering honestly the questions in the lessons, I understood that my own walk had blind spots that needed to be addressed in order for me to grow closer to God. I challenge you to have the courage of a warrior and to use this study to examine your own walk.

Enjoy the study and your journey as you discover just what it takes to become a warrior for Christ. Challenge yourself and those in your group to answer the questions without fear or judgment. Decide for yourself today that you will finish what you have started and learn as much as possible from God's Word. See you on the high ground.

– Col. Joel Hardin, USA (Ret.)

FOR SEVERAL YEARS, I have been a part of a men's group that meets weekly. We took turns leading this study, and God used it to draw us closer to Him and to each other. We signed the covenant as a group and made copies for each other. Mine is on my study wall, reminding me of my commitments to God, others, family, and self.

– Bob Liu; Belton, Texas

EVAN TRINKLE AND PASTOR STEVE Gehring have done us men a great service with this study. It is an encouraging, challenging, and practical Bible Study that gets at the issues that men need to deal with. I recommend it to every men's ministry and to every man who is serious about helping other men walk with the Lord and, as applicable, to be the husbands, fathers, and friends that God designed and called us to be. A great study to help disciples make disciples in our homes, churches and communities…exactly what Jesus commanded us to do!

– Greg Williams, Director, Kentucky Marriage Movement
The Family Foundation

I HAVE HAD THE PRIVILEGE of knowing both authors of this Bible study. I know them to be men who have a heart for God and for men and their families. They are mature men who have lived out what they are writing about. I pray that this Bible study will give you the tools to walk this life with integrity and as a person who pleases God.

– Ken Groen, Retired Pastor, Des Moines, Iowa

Foreword

"The LORD is a warrior..."
Exodus 15:3 (NET)

THE MAKING OF A SPIRITUAL WARRIOR Bible study and its designated parts outline a process that will shape, mold, forge, and transform your daily life with God. The study is broken down into the following four parts:

Part 1: Study the Warrior Covenant.

Part 2: Study the foundations of daily faith symbolized through the Warrior Ring.

Part 3: Conduct a covenant-signing ceremony and ring ceremony to mark the commitment made before God and others. Frame and display the covenant in a location of choice to serve as a daily reminder. Wear and share with others the Warrior Ring as a daily reminder of the covenant you made to God and before others.

Part 4: Live as a modern-day warrior. Share your hope and faith with others. Using the ring and covenant as an opportunity to talk and share with others should become a lifestyle that flows through each man and is seen by others.

The Warrior Covenant is a summation of "I will" pledges that a man makes and incorporates into his daily life. It is organized into four relationship categories: God, Family, Others, and Self. For each pledge, the Word of God (the Bible or Scriptures) reveals how a man should live his life to prosper (be successful) and be in right relationship with God, family, and others. The Warrior Covenant speaks of a man's covenantal relationship with God.

The Warrior Ring, discussed in part two, serves as a daily reminder of the pledge a man has made concerning his relationship with God. Six major themes that are tied to foundational principles represented in the Christian man's life are represented on the ring. Those themes are "Why Jesus and the Cross," "Death to Self through the Tomb and Baptism," "Empowerment of the Holy Spirit," "Producing Fruit in Our Lives," "Daily Vigilance (the Full Armor of God)," and "Daily Surrender." We will look deeper at these meanings later in the study.

It is my greatest desire for your life to be transformed by this study, whether through personal encounters and responses to the challenging questions or just by listening to responses of others around you if involved in a group study setting. My passion is that you will be a man after God's own heart. Allow yourself to be influenced by the Word of God. Let the Holy Spirit of God give you guidance, wisdom, and instruction to navigate successfully through your daily life. It is essential to humble yourself in order to receive all that God has for you through this study.

Since becoming a Christian, I have realized that every one of us was born with a God-given purpose in life that is fulfilled as you walk daily in a relationship with God, family, and others. Your birth was no accident. Even if the circumstances of your birth seem unplanned, nothing escapes the observation of God. Your birthday is a reminder of the day that was crafted for you. Recognizing this truth is powerful and brings an accompanying confidence. You are special, and no one else is like you. Each one of us was created to have a relationship with God. The Heavenly Father loves each of us even if it seems hard for us to comprehend His love. Yes, you are loved unconditionally. This covenant relationship with God is to be lived out daily.

Our life is not defined by our past unless we choose to live in the past. We make choices that can set a new course for our life. The right choices create a wonderful dynamic in our relationship with God. If our life is a wreck because of the choices we have made, then God can make our life new. If it was already good, He can make it better. He turns ashes into beauty, and He renews our life when we yield to Him. By yielding our life to God, we can experience a fresh starting point in our life. We don't have to be bound by our current circumstances.

Every man's life consists of a journey that will present many crossroads, options, or choices. These intersections in life can be challenging. Often they become defining moments in our life that take us down a road we never intended to travel. Based on one's choices, the result can be a blessing or a curse, good or evil, increase or decrease. Let this study be a starting point in your life, from which you will make wise decisions that will impact your life in a positive way.

Life is not about how you start, but how you finish!

Through Christ,

Evan

Introduction

"The LORD is a warrior..."
Exodus 15:3 (NET)

THE WARRIOR COVENANT AND Warrior Ring symbolize a daily covenant made to humanity by God as revealed in Scripture. The promises that God made with the ancient Israelites apply to all Christians today. Promises were made not only from God to humanity, but also from humanity to God. The relationship is not just one-sided; it is interactive, fresh, and renewed every day. The relationship with God is full of commitment and creates an unconditional bond between the parties in the covenant. When God says that He loves you, He loves you. We respond by loving Him. This relationship grows over time and becomes stronger the more one commits to it and gives oneself to it. The bond grows during both good and bad experiences. These experiences make the relationship stronger, the covenant firmer, and dependence on God more vital. Nothing can separate the love God has for you.

What is a covenant? In its simplest definition, it is a promise, an agreement between two or more parties. Unlike a contract, which is based on a relationship of mistrust, a covenant is based on a relationship of trust. Why a covenant? A covenant defines the intimate relationship that the living God of the universe wants to have with His people. Covenants lay out agreements between or promises made by those entering into the pledge. A covenant states what each party will do for his portion of the covenant (Deuteronomy 7:12-16). One of the most notable covenants in the Old Testament is the promise to Abraham that his descendants would multiply and inherit the land of Israel (Genesis 12:1-3, 15:1-21; Hebrews 6:13-16). Then in the New Testament, Jesus' death established a new covenant between God and humanity (Jeremiah 31:31-34; Mark 14:22-25; John 3:5-8; 1 Corinthians 11:23-26; Hebrews 8:6-13, 9:15-17).

All of us make covenants. Today they include promises or pledges between people. For example, both individuals in a marriage make a promise or pledge to remain together for the rest of their lives. Buying a house or a parcel of land is another example of entering into a contract. When we make a pledge, we make a serious commitment to our future behavior.

God is calling every one of us into a covenant with Him. He desires for us to live our lives following the example of His Son, Jesus Christ of Nazareth, as found in the Bible. God has removed the mystery of the covenant by providing a how-to book for all to read and an example for all to pattern their lives after. We can be mentored by learning from the life Jesus lived. We need to come to Him with a humble, surrendered heart and attitude. God wants our lives to be full and fulfilled. Our lives don't have to be filled with consuming anxiousness.

We cannot escape God in our lives. We may choose to ignore Him, as I did for many years, but He does not go away. The Scripture passages found throughout this study will show you just how intimate the relationship that God wants to have with you can be and how close you are already to God's heart. Walk with me through the pages to come and discover the life that God has planned for you. Learn how dynamic your days can be as you embark on a journey that will change your life forever.

Guidelines for Small Groups

THE FOLLOWING GUIDELINES WILL benefit both you and all participants in the Bible study. They will make your experience more enriching and provide a more open environment in which to learn and grow. Please review all of the guidelines so that all in the group understand them as foundational to the group.

CONFIDENTIALITY

It is critical that all in the group understand the importance of privacy. As the group progresses through the study, the leader will ask that members share their thoughts and feelings about the material. Those thoughts and feelings may relate to individuals' personal lives and will be shared out of trust that the group members will keep private what is shared inside the group, unless the members permit it to be shared outside the group. So please strictly honor and protect the confidence of members in the group.

RESPECT

As group members begin to share their personal thoughts, feelings, and opinions, don't judge. We all come from different life experiences, and God molds and purposes each of our lives differently. We can learn from each other if openness is encouraged and maintained. Not everyone has to have the same perspective on all points discussed. We all make up the body of Christ. Romans 12:4-5 (TLB) says, *"Just as there are many parts to our bodies, so it is with Christ's body. We are all parts of it, and it takes every one of us to make it complete, for we each have different work to do. So we belong to each other, and each needs all the others."*

PREPARATION

This study will be a journey, and to get the most from the experience, you need to be prepared. Commit to attending each of the meetings and read as much of the material as possible before coming. Write down the thoughts God reveals to you in private, so you can contribute during the group meeting. Your input is instrumental both to your growth and to the growth of the group members. We learn from each other, and as God stretches each member, all will mature and become more like Him.

ACCOUNTABILITY TO THE GROUP

It is no mistake that you are involved with this Bible study. It will play a significant part in your growth as a man of God—a man after God's own heart. Everything that is worthwhile takes commitment. Be steadfast and allow yourself to be transformed by the renewing of your mind and life through this study.

A Letter to Leaders

THANK YOU FOR HAVING A heart for ministry, specifically small group Bible study. This study's focus is on men and is designed to be encouraging and to challenge men to grow into what God's plan and purpose is for their lives.

Your role is to facilitate an environment where learning takes place—where men can share their ideas in a respectful environment. Draw men into discussion through the use of engaging questions and through listening to their responses.

You may feel nervous or unqualified to lead the group, but be encouraged: you are not alone. God equips those He calls. Be sensitive to the leading of the Holy Spirit as members of the group share their thoughts and feelings. Remind all to follow the guidelines set for the study.

Finally, prepare yourself. Read and study the material. Take time to mark which questions you feel led to discuss. You won't be able to cover every question if you pressure yourself to follow a timeline. It may take a week or more to cover a section. We encourage you to use the following guidelines to gauge the progression: Is learning taking place? Are men discussing the materials? Are they engaged? If they are, then move as fast or slow as the group determines.

Enjoy the study yourself and allow God to grow you from the materials and group interaction. We all grow as we listen and learn from each other. Allow God to use you and to speak through your life. Once again, thank you for your heart.

Abbreviations

for Old Testament and New Testament Books

OLD TESTAMENT

Genesis . . . . Gen.	2 Chronicles . . . . 2 Chr.	Daniel . . . . Dan.
Exodus . . . . Ex.	Ezra . . . . Ezra	Hosea . . . . Hos.
Leviticus . . . . Lev.	Nehemiah . . . . Neh.	Joel . . . . Joel
Numbers . . . . Num.	Esther . . . . Esth.	Amos . . . . Amos
Deuteronomy . . . . Deut.	Job . . . . Job	Obadiah . . . . Obad.
Joshua . . . . Josh.	Psalms . . . . Ps.	Jonah . . . . Jon.
Judges . . . . Judg.	Proverbs . . . . Prov.	Micah . . . . Mic.
Ruth . . . . Ruth	Ecclesiastes . . . . Eccl.	Nahum . . . . Nah.
1 Samuel . . . . 1 Sam.	Song of Solomon . . . . Song.	Habakkuk . . . . Hab.
2 Samuel . . . . 2 Sam.	Isaiah . . . . Is.	Zephaniah . . . . Zeph.
1 Kings . . . . 1 Kin.	Jeremiah . . . . Jer.	Haggai . . . . Hag.
2 Kings . . . . 2 Kin.	Lamentations . . . . Lam.	Zechariah . . . . Zech.
1 Chronicles . . . . 1 Chr.	Ezekiel . . . . Ezek.	Malachi . . . . Mal.

NEW TESTAMENT:

Matthew . . . . Matt.	Ephesians . . . . Eph.	Hebrews . . . . Heb.
Mark . . . . Mark	Philippians . . . . Phil.	James . . . . James
Luke . . . . Luke	Colossians . . . . Col.	1 Peter . . . . 1 Pe.
John . . . . John	1 Thessalonians . . . 1 Thess.	2 Peter . . . . 2 Pe.
Acts . . . . Acts	2 Thessalonians . . . 2 Thess.	1 John . . . . 1 John
Romans . . . . Rom.	1 Timothy . . . . 1 Tim.	2 John . . . . 2 John
1 Corinthians . . . . . . 1 Cor.	2 Timothy . . . . 2 Tim.	3 John . . . . 3 John
2 Corinthians . . . . . . 2 Cor.	Titus . . . . Titus	Jude . . . . Jude
Galatians . . . . Gal.	Philemon . . . . Philem.	Revelation . . . . Rev.

References

Bible Translations

King James Version . . . . KJV

New King James Version . . . . NKJV

New International Version . . . . NIV

English Standard Version . . . . ESV

Living Bible . . . . TLB

Amplified Bible . . . . AMP

New American Standard . . . . NASB

New English Translation . . . . NET

Holman Christian Standard Bible . . . . HCSB

Modern English Version . . . . MEV

New American Standard Bible 1977 . . . . NASB77

Helpful Bible Study Websites

Blue Letter Bible . . . . www.blueletterbible.org

Bible Hub . . . . www.biblehub.com

Bible Questions Answered . . . . www.gotquestions.org

Christian Truth . . . . www.compellingtruth.org

Study Outline

The Warrior Covenant and Warrior Ring

"The Lord is a warrior..."
Exodus 15:3 (NET)

Study of the Warrior Covenant — Part 1

Study of the Warrior Ring — Part 2

The Warrior Covenant

"The Lord is a warrior…" (Exodus 15:3, NET)

God

I will, with all my understanding, love the Lord with all of my heart, soul, mind, and strength and have no other gods before the Lord my God. Ex. 20:3; Deut. 6:5; Mark 12:30

I will seek the Lord, His kingdom, and His righteousness first and foremost and then worship nothing other than the Lord God. Ex. 20:4; Deut. 4:35 (ESV); Is. 44:6 (ESV); Matt. 6:33; Rom. 1:25, 3:10-12, 21-24, 5:12-21, 12:1-2; 2 Cor. 5:21; James 1:14, 4:4; 1 John 2:15-17

I will follow, honor, and submit to the plans and purposes designed by God for my life. Gen. 1:28; Ps. 139:1-18, 23-24; Eccl. 12:13; Is. 43:7; Jer. 29:11-13; Micah 6:8; John 4:23, 15:16; 1 Cor. 6:19-20; Eph. 1:4-12, 2:9-10; Phil. 3:9-10

Family

I will honor my mother and father and all authority placed over my life. Ex. 20:12; Deut. 27:16a; Lev. 19:3a; Matt. 15:4; Rom. 13:1-7; Eph. 6:1-3; 1 Tim. 2:1-2; Titus 3:1; 1 Pet. 2:13-17

I will love, honor, and cherish my marriage and my wife. Deut. 5:18; Prov. 12:4a; 18:22; Eph. 5:25-33; Col. 3:19; Heb.13:4; 1 Pet. 3:7

I will, if I have children, intentionally teach and, by God's grace and power, model the Word of God. Deut. 6:6-7, 11:18-31; Prov. 22:6; Col. 3:21

Others

I will love and treat my neighbor the way I would like to be treated. Mark 12:31; Luke 6:27-42; Rom. 13:8-10; Gal. 5:13-15; James 2:8-9; 1 John 4:7-21

I will not allow my liberty or freedom in Christ to be a stumbling block to others, neither judging them nor causing others to fall away, lose faith, or blaspheme God because of my liberty. Rom. 14:12-23; 1 Cor. 8:4-13, 10:23-30; Gal. 5:13-14

I will be accountable to other men, to my wife, and to my family. Prov. 13:20, 17:17, 18:1, 27:17; Gal. 5:15-21, 6:1-5; 1 Thess. 5:11-15; Heb. 10:24-25; James 5:16

Self

I will seek knowledge, wisdom, discernment, and understanding. 1 Kings 3:9-12; Prov. 2:1-8, 3:13, 4:20-22, 19:20; Matt. 7:7-8; James 1:5-6

I will put off completely my selfish, sinful life and put on the new life found in Christ Jesus and submit to the renewing of my mind, that He might sanctify me, having cleansed me by the washing of water with the Word. Rom. 12:1-2; Eph. 4:22-24, 5:26; Col. 3:8-17; James 1:21; 2 Cor. 5:17-19; Phil. 4:8-9

I will by God's grace commit to being patient and kind; not jealous, boastful, proud or rude; not demanding my own way; not irritable or keeping records of wrong; not taking part in injustice; not being self-willed, quick-tempered, or violent; not being greedy but hospitable, sober-minded, just, and self-controlled. 1 Cor. 13:4-7; Gal. 5:22-23; 1 Tim. 3:8-13; Titus 1:5-9

I will daily live by the Word of God through the power of the Holy Spirit. Ps. 19:7-14, 111:10, 119:2, 11, 97-98, 130, 105; Matt. 4:4; 2 Tim. 3:16-17; Heb. 4:12-13

I will listen to and seek counsel from the Holy Spirit. 1 Chr. 28:9; Prov. 8:1-19; Luke 2:25-27a, 4:1, 11:9-13; Rom. 8:26-27; 1 Jn. 2:27, 5:14

I will daily put on the armor of God. 2 Cor. 10:3-6; Eph. 6:10-18

I will set no unclean thing before my eyes, and I will flee from lust and sexual immorality. Job 31:1, 4; Ps. 119:11; Prov. 6:23-29; Matt. 5:27-28; 1 Cor. 3:16, 7:1, 8, 26, 32; Eph. 5:8-17; Phil. 4:8

I, _____, pledge before God this _____ day of _____ , 20___, to make every effort to walk in His grace, with integrity, allowing Him to make me into a man who reflects the image of Christ Jesus for the glory of God.

"The Lord is a warrior..."
Exodus 15:3 (NET)

Part 1: The Warrior Covenant

Lesson 1
Our Covenant With God

WHAT IS A *COVENANT*? In its simplest definition, it is a promise, an agreement between two or more parties. Unlike a contract, which is based on a relationship of mistrust, a covenant is based on a relationship of trust. Why a covenant? A covenant defines the intimate relationship that the living God of the universe wants to have with His people. Covenants lay out agreements between or promises by those entering into the pledge of what each will do for his part of the covenant (Deuteronomy 7:12-16). One of the most notable covenants in the Old Testament is God's promise to Abraham that his descendants would multiply and inherit the land of Israel (Genesis 12:1-3, 15:1-21, Hebrews 6:13-16). Then in the New Testament, Jesus' death established a new covenant between God and humanity (Jeremiah 31:31-34; Mark 14:22-25; John 3:5-8; 1 Corinthians 11:23-26; Hebrews 8:6-13, 9:15-17).

All of us make covenants. Today they are promises or pledges between people. For example, both individuals in a marriage make a promise or pledge to remain together for the rest of their lives. Buying a house or a parcel of land is another example of entering into a contract. When we make a pledge, we are making a serious commitment to our future behavior.

Today God is calling every one of us into a covenant with Him. He desires for us to live our lives after the example of His Son, Jesus Christ of Nazareth, as found in the Bible. God has removed the mystery of the covenant by providing a how-to book for all to read and an example for us to pattern our lives after. We can be mentored by learning from the life Jesus lived. We need to come to Him with a humble, surrendered heart and attitude. God wants our lives to be full and fulfilled. Our lives don't have to be filled with consuming anxiousness.

I will, with all my understanding, love the Lord with all of my heart, soul, mind, and strength and have no other gods before the Lord my God. Ex. 20:3, Deut. 6:5, Mark 12:30

We live in a culture and time in history where it seems that everything but God is important. Instead of worshipping God first and making His principles the guiding rule in our life, we allow culture to gain more influence than the lifestyle designed by God found in the Bible. The Scripture passage found in **1 John 2:15-17** (TLB) says:

> *Stop loving this evil world and all that it offers you, for when you love these things you show that you do not really love God; ¹⁶for all these worldly things, these evil desires—the craze for sex, the ambition to buy everything that appeals to you, and the pride that comes from wealth and importance—these are not from God. They are from this evil world itself. ¹⁷And this world is fading away, and these evil, forbidden things will go with it, but whoever keeps doing the will of God will live forever.*

You will never be satisfied if your attentions are focused on everything around you. There will always be something else that you don't have. You will constantly be pulled to yield and to pursue something or someone other than God.

DISCUSSION

Deuteronomy 6:5 (NKJV) says:

> *You shall love the Lord your God with all your heart, with all your soul, and with all your strength.*

Question: What does it mean to you, to have no other gods besides Him? (Additional reference Isaiah 44:6.)

Study Notes

_____

_____

_____

_____

_____

DISCUSSION

Question: What are some "other gods" that you may have in your life?

Study Notes

_____

_____

_____

_____

_____

_____

_____

_____

DISCUSSION

Question: What makes it tough for you to get rid of these "other gods"?

Study Notes

_____

_____

_____

_____

_____

_____

_____

_____

DISCUSSION

Questions: Life is a matter not just of balance, but of priorities. Each day you make decisions. To what am I surrendering? If the Lord is your God, do you bow and submit to Him in all of your decisions? What about your family, job, and money? Are you daily placing them at the feet of the Lord? Is everything you have, all of your dreams and hopes, placed at the feet of the Lord? If not, why not? What is your struggle?

Study Notes

_____

_____

_____

_____

_____

Application: Ancient Israel was instructed by God to once a year cleanse their houses of leaven.

Exodus 12:15 (AMP) says:

> *[In celebration of the Passover in future years] seven days shall you eat unleavened bread; even the first day you shall put away leaven [symbolic of corruption] out of your houses; for whoever eats leavened bread from the first day until the seventh day, that person shall be cut off from Israel.*

Today we should be just as diligent to guard our houses and lives from corruption, from any unwanted influences either deliberately or un-deliberately brought into our life. Ask yourself if you have opened yourself up to unhealthy influences. Are you chasing pursuits that are not aligned with God's desires? Have you substituted something or someone before God? Examining your priorities and choices is something you need to do regularly. We have annual examinations at the doctor's office to look for any new developments in our overall health condition. We need to practice daily and annual spiritual checkups with God.

Hebrews 11:6 (MEV) says:

> *And without faith it is impossible to please God, for he who comes to God must believe that He exists and that He is a rewarder of those who diligently seek Him.*

What is the source of your reward? Are you blessed and rewarded by God, or are you allowing something else to take God's place?

I will seek the Lord, His kingdom, and His righteousness first and foremost and then worship nothing other than the Lord God. Ex. 20:4; Deut. 4:35 (ESV); Is. 44:6 (ESV); Matt. 6:33; Rom. 1:25, 3:10-12, 21-24, 5:12-21, 12:1-2; 2 Cor. 5:21; James 1:14, 4:4; 1 John 2:15-17

While serving with the military in Iraq, I met a man named Jim (not his real name) who said to me one day, "I've been watching you. You're different. What makes you different?"

To this question I replied, "Do you really want to know?" He said that he did want to know, so for the next two hours, I explained to him how God, through Jesus' sacrifice on the cross and the life Jesus lived on earth, had completely changed my life once I surrendered to Him and to the plan He had for my life. Well, Jim and I agreed to meet and study the Bible to discover what it might reveal to him and how it could change his life too. After weeks of study and discussion, Jim admitted that he needed to change his life, but Jim was struggling with letting go of the lifestyle patterns and choices to which he had become so accustomed. He just wouldn't let go of his past for God's promise of a better future. Unfortunately, even to this day Jim has not let go of his lifestyle and chosen God's best. Many are like Jim. They know God is real and that He has a better plan for their life, but they just can't let go and trust God completely for their future life.

DISCUSSION

1 John 2:15-17 (MEV) says:

> *Do not love the world or the things in the world. If anyone loves the world, the love of the Father is not in him. [16]For all that is in the world—the lust of the flesh, the lust of the eyes, and the pride of life—is not of the Father, but is of the world. [17]The world and its desires are passing away, but the one who does the will of God lives forever..*

Questions: What is so captivating about the world's ways that a person desires them more than following Jesus' example? How is the Lord's way different from the world's way? What are some ways we can be in this world but not of this world?

Matthew 6:33 (MEV) say:

> *But seek first the kingdom of God and His righteousness, and all these things shall be given to you.*

Study Notes

_____

_____

_____

_____

_____

_____

_____

DISCUSSION

Romans 12:1, 2 (MEV) says:

I urge you therefore, brothers, by the mercies of God, that you present your bodies as a living sacrifice, holy, and acceptable to God, which is your reasonable service of worship. [2]Do not be conformed to this world, but be transformed by the renewing of your mind, that you may prove what is the good and acceptable and perfect will of God.

Questions: How do you understand being in the world, but not being a part of the world? How do you demonstrate to others around you what it looks like to live in the world but not be a part of it? What are some things that you have had to give up in order to avoid conforming to the world? What has God used to bring about a transformation in your life?

Study Notes

_____

_____

_____

_____

_____

_____

DISCUSSION

How do you define *righteousness*?

Romans 3:10-12 (NASB77) says:

> as it is written, "THERE IS NONE RIGHTEOUS, NOT EVEN ONE; [11]THERE IS NONE WHO UNDERSTANDS, THERE IS NONE WHO SEEKS FOR GOD; [12]ALL HAVE TURNED ASIDE, TOGETHER THEY HAVE BECOME USELESS; THERE IS NONE WHO DOES GOOD, THERE IS NOT EVEN ONE."

Romans 3:21-24 (NASB77) says:

> *But now apart from the Law the righteousness of God has been manifested, being witnessed by the Law and the Prophets, [22]even the righteousness of God through faith in Jesus Christ for all those who believe; for there is no distinction; [23]for all have sinned and fall short of the glory of God, [24]being justified as a gift by His grace through the redemption which is in Christ Jesus.*

Questions: According to the Bible, can you have righteousness in your own abilities or decisions? What does righteousness mean to you based on these Scriptures? Do you have a different perspective of righteousness now that you have studied these passages? How does Jesus make it possible for you to have right standing before God the Father?

Study Notes

_____

_____

_____

_____

_____

Application: A total commitment causes you to seek with all of your energies obtaining the satisfaction of capturing your objective—winning the prize. A singular focus is given to the process, and you are not easily distracted from your desire. Daily choices reflect your devotion to serving God. Worshipping Him results from your priorities. Daily decisions, incrementally applied over time, produces a transformed life. Decisions matter, and they make a tremendous impact on both our life and the lives of others around us. When your priorities are right, your life reflects Jesus, and the Holy Spirit living through you will draw others to God.

I will follow, honor, and submit to the plans and purposes designed by God for my life. Gen. 1:28; Ps. 139:1-18, 23-24; Eccl. 12:13; Is. 43:7; Jer. 29:11-13; Micah 6:8; Jn. 4:23, 15:16; 1 Cor. 6:19-20; Eph. 1:4-12, 2:9-10; Phil. 3:9-10

One's life purpose gives direction and helps a person navigate through the many daily choices that he faces. Thomas Carlyle, a Scottish philosopher, essayist, historian, and teacher said, "A man without a purpose is like a ship without a rudder—a waif, a nothing, a no man. Have a purpose in life, and, having it, throw such strength of mind and muscle into your work as God has given you." Yield to the plan designed for your life. There is no one like you, and God designed you uniquely. God has equipped you to fulfill all that you have been called to do, so it is not that you are unqualified—just unwilling. Billy Sunday, the celebrated and influential American evangelist, said, "More men fail through lack of purpose than lack of talent." John Wesley, a seventeenth-century Anglican minister, theologian, and the founder of Methodism, said, "I want the whole Christ for my Savior, the whole Bible for my book, the whole Church for my fellowship, and the whole world for my mission field." All of life is before you, and you don't have to walk through life alone. According to Psalm 139, God knew you before you were ever born. As you continue on this journey, you will discover all that God has for you!

DISCUSSION

Jeremiah 29:11-13 (NASB77) says:

> *"For I know the plans that I have for you," declares the LORD, "plans for welfare and not for calamity to give you a future and a hope. [12]Then you will call upon Me and come and pray to Me, and I will listen to you. [13]And you will seek Me and find Me, when you search for Me with all your heart."*

Questions: Do you believe God has a plan for your life? How can you know God's plan and purpose? Do you see that only you can fulfill your place in the body of Christ? You're a puzzle piece that fits into the entire picture of God.

Study Notes

_____

_____

_____

_____

_____

_____

_____

_____

DISCUSSION

Genesis 1:28 (NKJV) says:

Then God blessed them, and God said to them, "Be fruitful and multiply; fill the earth and subdue it; have dominion over the fish of the sea, over the birds of the air, and over every living thing that moves on the earth.

Ecclesiastes 12:13 (NASB77) says:

The conclusion, when all has been heard, is: fear God and keep His commandments, because this applies to every person.

Isaiah 43:7 (NKJV) says:

Everyone who is called by My name, Whom I have created for My glory; I have formed him, yes, I have made him.

Micah 6:8 (AMP) says:

He has showed you, O man, what is good. And what does the Lord require of you but to do justly, and to love kindness and mercy, and to humble yourself and walk humbly with your God?

John 4:23 (MEV) says:

Yet the hour is coming, and is now here, when the true worshipers will worship the Father in spirit and truth. For the Father seeks such to worship Him.

John 15:16 (NKJV) says:

You did not choose Me, but I chose you and appointed you that you should go and bear fruit, and that your fruit should remain, that whatever you ask the Father in My name He may give you.

1 Corinthians 6:19, 20 (AMP) says:

"Do you not know that your body is the temple (the very sanctuary) of the Holy Spirit Who lives within you, Whom you have received [as a Gift] from God? You are not your own, [20]You were bought with a price [purchased with a preciousness and paid for, made His own]. So then, honor God and bring glory to Him in your body."

Philippians 3:9-10 (AMP) says:

"And that I may [actually] be found and known as in Him, not having any [self-achieved] righteousness that can be called my own, based on my obedience to the Law's demands (ritualistic uprightness and supposed right standing with God thus acquired), but possessing that [genuine righteousness] which comes through faith in Christ (the Anointed One), the [truly] right standing with God, which comes from God by [saving] faith. [10][For my determined purpose is] that I may know Him [that I may progressively become more deeply and intimately acquainted with Him, perceiving and recognizing and understanding the wonders of His Person more strongly and more clearly], and that I may in that same way come to know the power out flowing from His resurrection [which it exerts over believers], and that I may so share His sufferings as to be continually transformed [in spirit into His likeness even] to His death, [in the hope]"

Ephesians 2:10 (AMP) says:

"For we are God's [own] handiwork (His workmanship), recreated in Christ Jesus, [born anew] that we may do those good works which God predestined (planned beforehand) for us [taking paths which He prepared ahead of time], that we should walk in them [living the good life which He prearranged and made ready for us to live].

Ephesians 1:4-12 (NASB77) says:

"just as He chose us in Him before the foundation of the world, that we should be holy and blameless before Him. In love [5]He predestined us to adoption as sons through Jesus Christ to Himself, according to the kind intention of His will, [6]to the praise of the glory of His grace, which He freely bestowed on us in the Beloved. [7]In Him we have redemption through His blood, the forgiveness of our trespasses, according to the riches of His grace, [8]which He lavished upon us. In all wisdom and insight [9]He made known to us the mystery of His will, according to His kind intention which He purposed in Him [10]with a view to an administration suitable to the fulness of the times, that is, the summing up of all things in Christ, things in the heavens and things upon the earth. In Him [11]also we have obtained an inheritance, having been predestined according to His

purpose who works all things after the counsel of His will, [12]to the end that we who were the first to hope in Christ should be to the praise of His glory."

Questions: What do these passages reveal about your purpose? Consider God's purpose for you. What has He called you to do?

Study Notes

_____

_____

_____

_____

_____

_____

_____

Application: The world's way is for you to be your own person, a self-made man. All you have to do is strive to become smarter or more talented. This way doesn't come without a cost. You struggle to achieve and slowly lose a tenderness for following the lead of the Holy Spirit in your life. You trust only in yourself and in what you can control. You try to pattern your life after what the ungodly world system suggests success looks like. There's no focus on Jesus, just a focus on you. You start replacing God with things, and your relationship with God grows cold and distant. Loving the world more than God is not worth it; the cost is too high. Be encouraged. God is faithful, and He will always walk with you.

You may not have a clue what God's plan and purpose is for your life. The future may look like a complete mystery. Abraham too was in that same place. He had to trust in the One Who was trustworthy. Daily he had to walk out the journey. You can't escape having to walk out your daily purpose. If you could skip the daily trusting and sacrifice, going directly to "GO" (like on the board game Monopoly), you would miss growing in your faith and learning to trust your Heavenly Father. You would not develop confidence, and you would miss steadfastness in your life. Your life is unique! I can't live your life for you, nor do I want to, but I do want to encourage you to rest and to avoid striving to make something happen in your life when you should be patiently waiting for God to move in your life. He knew you before you were ever born, so He also knows that you are special and wonderfully made. Rest and don't rush anything.

God remained faithful to Abraham, consistently showing Abraham that He was faithful. God will be faithful to you also as you daily surrender and develop a stronger trust. Surrendering your plans and dreams to His purposes is not an easy thing to do, but when you surrender, a quiet peace and joy fill your heart, along with God's promises found in Scripture. The main difference in your life is Jesus and the Holy Spirit's living through you. When you completely surrender all of your life to the Lordship of Jesus Christ, nothing will stop the fulfillment of God's plan and purpose for your life.

Further Study

Read Psalm 33:18-22; Isaiah 64:4-8; Romans 8:1-10; and 2 Corinthians 5:21. Look at Hebrews 11:1-40. What can you learn from others' practice of faith? Read Genesis 12:4-9. Will you leave your past behind you as Abraham left his? James 1:5 and 17, 2:5, and 5:7 reflect the value of patiently waiting on God in your life. *The Pursuit of God*, written by A.W. Tozer, may be of interest to you for further reading.

NOTES:

_____

_____

_____

_____

_____

_____

_____

_____

_____

_____

_____

_____

_____

_____

_____

_____

"The Lord is a warrior..."
Exodus 15:3 (NET)

Part 1: The Warrior Covenant

Lesson 2
Our Covenant With Family

I will honor my mother and father and all authority placed over my life. Ex. 20:12; Deut. 27:16a; Lev. 19:3a; Matt. 15:4; Rom. 13:1-7; Eph. 6:1-3; 1 Tim. 2:1, 2; Titus 3:1; 1 Pet. 2:13-17

THERE IS AN INTERESTING story among Grimm's fairytales of a son and his wife and their treatment of their aging father. The thought-provoking story reveals their heart. What is comforting is that their hearts changed. According to the story, there was once a little old man whose eyes blinked and hands trembled; when he ate, he clattered the silverware distressingly, missed his mouth with the spoon as often as not, and dribbled a bit of his food on the tablecloth. He lived with his married son, having nowhere else to live, and his son's wife did not like the arrangement.

"I can't have this," she said. "It interferes with my right to happiness." So she and her husband took the old man gently, but firmly, by the arm and led him to the corner of the kitchen. There they set him on a stool and gave him his food in an earthenware bowl. From then on, he always ate in the corner, blinking at the table with wistful eyes.

One day his hands trembled rather more than usual, and the earthenware bowl fell and broke. "If you are a pig," said the daughter-in-law, "you must eat out of a trough." So they made him a little wooden trough and gave him his meals in that.

These people had a four-year-old son of whom they were very fond. One evening the young man noticed his boy playing intently with some bits of wood and asked what he was doing.

"I'm making a trough," he said, smiling up for approval, "to feed you and Mamma out of when I get big."

The man and his wife looked at each other for a while and didn't say anything. Then they cried a little. They then went to the corner, took the old man by the arm, and led him back to the table.

– 41 –

They sat him in a comfortable chair and gave him his food on a plate, and from then on, nobody ever scolded when he clattered or spilled or broke things.

Honoring someone is a willful action on your part. You both initiate honor and give it freely. Honor shows great respect and admiration toward someone.

DISCUSSION

Romans 13:1-7 (MEV) says:

> Let every person be subject to the governing authorities, for there is no authority except from God, and those that exist are appointed by God. [2]Therefore whoever resists the authority resists what God has appointed, and those who resist will incur judgment. [3]Rulers are not a terror to good works, but to evil works. Do you wish to have no fear of the authority? Do what is good, and you will have praise from him, for he is the servant of God for your good. But if you do what is evil, be afraid, for he does not bear the sword in vain, [4]for he is the servant of God, an avenger to execute wrath upon him who practices evil. [5]So it is necessary to be in subjection, not only because of wrath, but also for the sake of conscience. [6]For this reason you also pay taxes, for they are God's servants, devoting themselves to this very thing. [7]Render to all what is due them: taxes to whom taxes are due, respect to whom respect is due, fear to whom fear is due, and honor to whom honor is due.

Questions: What does it mean to honor someone? If the authority is bad, corrupt, or abusive, how should you treat them? Does God make mistakes by allowing ungodly authority over our lives? Is there any difference between how you should treat any kind of authority?

Study Notes

_____

_____

_____

_____

_____

_____

_____

DISCUSSION

1 Timothy 2:1, 2 (MEV) says:

Therefore I exhort first of all that you make supplications, prayers, intercessions, and thanksgivings for everyone, ²for kings and for all who are in authority, that we may lead a quiet and peaceful life in all godliness and honesty.

Titus 3:1-7 (TLB) says:

Remind your people to obey the government and its officers, and always to be obedient and ready for any honest work. ²They must not speak evil of anyone, nor quarrel, but be gentle and truly courteous to all. ³Once we, too, were foolish and disobedient; we were misled by others and became slaves to many evil pleasures and wicked desires. Our lives were full of resentment and envy. We hated others and they hated us. ⁴But when the time came for the kindness and love of God our Savior to appear, ⁵then he saved us—not because we were good enough to be saved but because of his kindness and pity—by washing away our sins and giving us the new joy of the indwelling Holy Spirit, ⁶whom he poured out upon us with wonderful fullness—and all because of what Jesus Christ our Savior did ⁷so that he could declare us good in God's eyes—all because of his great kindness; and now we can share in the wealth of the eternal life he gives us, and we are eagerly looking forward to receiving it.

1 Peter 2:13-15 (NASB77) says:

Submit yourselves for the Lord's sake to every human institution, whether to a king as the one in authority, or to governors as sent by him for the punishment of evildoers and the praise of those who do right. For such is the will of God that by doing right you may silence the ignorance of foolish men.

Questions: What are you instructed to do for your appointed leaders? Why? What are you modeling when you subject yourself to authority?

Study Notes

DISCUSSION

Exodus 20:12 (TLB) says:

Honor your father and mother, that you may have a long, good life in the land the Lord your God will give you.

Deuteronomy 27:16 (NKJV) says:

'Cursed is the one who treats his father or his mother with contempt.' "And all the people shall say, 'Amen!' "

Deuteronomy 27:16 (MEV) says:

"Cursed is he who disrespects his father or his mother." And all the people shall say, "Amen."

Ephesians 6:1-3 (TLB) says:

Children, obey your parents; this is the right thing to do because God has placed them in authority over you. ²Honor your father and mother. This is the first of God's Ten Commandments that ends with a promise. ³And this is the promise: that if you honor your father and mother, yours will be a long life, full of blessing.

Questions:Why do you think God included honoring your parents in the Ten Commandments? Should you treat your parents any differently than you do right now? Contempt is a strong word. What does it mean to you? Reflect and ask yourself if you are guilty of any contempt?

Study Notes

_____

_____

_____

_____

_____

_____

_____

Application: Everybody has parents. You can't escape your responsibility to them. You may not have had a great relationship with them, but you still have parents. By God's design, your parents are the first exposure you have to authority; therefore, they influence one's perception of God. Before you know anything about teachers, police officers, or local, state, and federal government officials, you have a parent or someone who acts in the role of a parent. Honoring (respecting and paying tribute) to your parent(s) brings a promise to your life. You might come from a broken, dysfunctional family background or from stable family conditions.

How you treat your parent(s) or the authority figures in your life reflects on how you honor God. If you have to forgive, then do so. If you need to ask forgiveness for how you've acted or for your attitude, then do it. God has forgiven you, so you should forgive others. If necessary, there is emotional and spiritual healing waiting for you as you take that step of forgiveness. Allow all of God's promises to flow through your life by first paying tribute to your parents and then to all other authorities in your life. Humble yourself if necessary. Please don't allow stubbornness or a lack of forgiveness to hamper you. Put the past behind you and move on to the wonderful plan God has waiting for you.

Further Study:

Deuteronomy 5:16	Proverbs 10:1; 13:1; 15:20	2 Timothy 3:1, 2

I will love, honor, and cherish my marriage and my wife. Deut. 5:18; Prov. 12:4a, 18:22; Eph. 5:25-33; Col. 3:19; Heb. 13:4; 1 Pet.3:7

I put together these definitions found in various dictionaries to provide some food for thought as we look at cherishing and honoring our wives.

Respect: "to esteem, admire, value, pay attention to, be considerate and thoughtful towards; to have a high opinion of (the opposite of respect is to disregard)"

Honor: "to esteem or exalt; to pay tribute to; to dignify; to keep a promise and fulfill (the opposite is dishonor)"

Love: "to adore, to feel affection for, to be devoted, to care for; to feel tender affection for or show kindness toward"

Cherish: "to treasure, value, prize, take pleasure in; to esteem"

DISCUSSION

Ephesians 5:25-33 (TLB) says:

And you husbands, show the same kind of love to your wives as Christ showed to the Church when he died for her, [26]to make her holy and clean, washed by baptism and God's Word; [27]so that he could give her to himself as a glorious Church without a single spot or wrinkle or any other blemish, being holy and without a single fault. [28]That is how husbands should treat their wives, loving them as parts of themselves. For since a man and his wife are now one, a man is really doing himself a favor and loving himself when he loves his wife! [29-30]No one hates his own body but lovingly cares for it, just as Christ cares for his body the Church, of which we are parts. [31](That the husband and wife are one body is proved by the Scripture, which says, "A man must leave his father and mother when he marries so that he can be perfectly joined to his wife, and the two shall be one.") [32]I know this is hard to understand, but it is an illustration of the way we are parts of the body of Christ. [33]So again I say, a man must love his wife as a part of himself; and the wife must see to it that she deeply respects her husband—obeying, praising, and honoring him.

Questions: What does it mean to cherish your marriage and wife? What can you say about the value, worth, or significance you place on your relationship with your wife? What actions and attitudes should you have toward your wife? Do you need to change anything with your wife?

Study Notes

_____

_____

_____

_____

_____

_____

_____

Questions: What does it mean to love your wife as Christ loved the church, the body of Christ? How do you see commitment? How does commitment shape your relationship with your wife and marriage?

Study Notes

_____

_____

_____

_____

_____

_____

_____

Application: If you are married, do you really cherish your relationship? The grass is not greener on the other side. Learn how to be tender towards your wife. Do not allow yourself to become bitter and demanding or hateful toward her. Prize, value, esteem, take pleasure in, and treasure her. Treat her with the highest regard. Are you giving yourself up for your wife?

Shouldn't you be sacrificing and placing her first as Jesus placed the church before Himself? Our wives trust us to provide a covering for them. Don't compromise that trust and integrity in your marriage for an adulterous relationship. That substitution only tears at the very fabric of God's very best for your life. Enjoy the fulfilling relationship with your wife. In return, be faithful and work at giving your very best to your wife, family, and God. Honor God by honoring your wife.

Further Study

Read Proverbs 5:18 and Ecclesiastes 9:9. When we realize that our days are numbered, how should we live each day with our wives? There are blessings given to you based on the way you treat your wife. Do you see your wife as your soul mate? She completes who you are. God gave you your wife to bless you.

Additional Thoughts

Heed these warnings, used by permission by Pastor Steve Pearson of Church of the Savior in Lexington, Kentucky.

ADULTERY WARNINGS

See: 2 Samuel 11-19, Proverbs 6:23-35; Proverbs 7:6-27

13 Judgments on Adultery

1. **Your children** will end up despising you because you abandoned them and broke their hearts. This is a most cruel thing. **Proverbs 17:6**, *"...the glory of children is their father."*

2. You will **experience shame** for the rest of your life because you broke the vow you made with your wife. She gave you the best years of her life, and then you treacherously abandoned her **Malachi 2:14-16; Ecclesiastes 5:4-5; Proverbs 5:18-23** .

3. God will **bring judgment** on you, and it will increase in intensity until you repent. **Hebrews 12:6** (NASB) says, *"For those whom the Lord loves he disciplines...."* He will chastise you on every level in order to get you to repent (Revelation 3:19).

4. You will lose **your reputation** as a man of character. Your reputation is your greatest asset. It takes a lifetime to build a reputation, and suddenly it will be gone. Instead, you will be known as a betrayer of those you once claimed to love. **Proverbs 22:1** (NASB) states clearly, *"A good name is to be more desired than great wealth..."* (or anything else). Why throw away your honor eternally for this?

5. You will damage **the Lord's reputation** and name by your actions. Since you have, told myriads of people that you are a servant of the Lord, you have now broken their trust by your duplicity and damaged their faith in God. You have broken the first commandment: *"You shall not take the name of the Lord your God in vain"* (**Exodus 20:7**). (You took His name in vain because you represent Him.)

6. You will lose your **place in ministry**, which is why God has left you on the earth. Your anointing will vanish, like Samson's strength. According to Judges 16:20, the spiritual gifts He gave you will go unused the rest of your life. He will demote you until you repent. **Psalm 75:7a** says, *"God is the judge."*

7. All **the people** the Lord destined for you to help in the future will go un-helped because you walked away and "checked out" from walking with God. There will be a huge vacuum, that you were meant to fill, that will go unfilled, like George Bailey's character in the movie, *It's a Wonderful Life* (**Ezekiel 22:30**).

8. You will **lose your health**. God will take away His hand of protection from you in order to get you to repent. You will be at Satan's mercy (**1 Samuel 15:22**). You will constantly experience unnecessary pressure because you disobeyed the Lord. You will not find rest. Isaiah 48:22 says there is no peace for the wicked. It is dangerous to disobey God (**Hebrews 6:4-6**).

9. You have walked into a demonic trap. **The woman** that you now claim to love is a disturbed, wicked, and treacherous person. No matter what she pretends to be, it is invalidated by the proof that she has joined and encouraged you in rebellion against God. You will be yoked to an immoral, unstable woman forever. **1 Corinthians 6:16** (NASB) says, *"Do you not know that the one who joins himself to a prostitute is one body with her?"*

10. **Your finances** will be judged. You will now be supporting two families. God will allow "the Devourer" to ravage your checkbook. God will not bless wickedness—ever (**Malachi 3:6-12**).

11. You have become **a stumbling block** to everyone, including your lover and everyone she knows. The collateral damage is beyond estimation. PLEASE pay attention to Jesus' words in **Matthew 18:6**.

12. You left your wife "in order to be happy." Actually, you will **never be happy** again because you will never recover from this on any level. The last years of a person's life are supposed to be their "best years." Instead, the last years of your life will be full of regret, tears, broken relationships, distrust, and suffering if adultery is the path you have chosen. If you are faithful to God, you will be happy, and He will give you a new love for your spouse. **Proverbs 6:32-33** (NASB) states, *"The one who commits adultery with a woman is lacking sense. He who would DESTROY*

HIMSELF does it. [33] Wounds and disgrace he will find, And his reproach will not be blotted out."

13. Most important of all, you will one day stand before **the judgment seat of Christ** and give an account for your choices. An adulterer's experience at the judgment seat will not be good (**2 Corinthians 5:10, 1 Corinthians 3:10-17**).

Repent now. Walk away. Get help before it's too late.

I will, if I have children, intentionally teach and, by God's grace and power, model the Word of God. Deut. 6:6-7; 11:18-31; Prov. 22:6; Col. 3:21

There is much to be said about parenting, and for many, it is a learn-as-you-go process filled with successes and mistakes. Too often parents are too hard on themselves. Remember the words of Anne Frank who said of children, "Parents can only give good advice or put them on the right paths, but the final forming of a person's character lies in their own hands." Our children bear responsibility too. H. W. Beecher once said, "You cannot teach a child to take care of himself unless you will let him take care of himself. He will make mistakes, and out of these mistakes will come his wisdom." Parents shape, mold, and then influence their children's lives. If this development is kept in balance, parenting is a smoother experience.

DISCUSSION

Deuteronomy 6:4-9 (NKJV) says:

> *Hear, O Israel: The LORD our God, the LORD is one!* ^{5}*You shall love the LORD your God with all your heart, with all your soul, and with all your strength.* ^{6}*And these words which I command you today shall be in your heart.* ^{7}*You shall teach them diligently to your children, and shall talk of them when you sit in your house, when you walk by the way, when you lie down, and when you rise up.* ^{8}*You shall bind them as a sign on your hand, and they shall be as frontlets between your eyes.* ^{9}*You shall write them on the doorposts of your house and on your gates.*

Questions: In your opinion, what character traits make parents good teachers for their children? Why should a father bother to teach his children? What is the value added to the time invested to intentionally teach your children? What do you want to reap from the effort?

Study Notes

_____

_____

_____

_____

_____

_____

DISCUSSION

Rearing children is much like farming. When you sow your seed into the ground, you don't know how fruitful the return will be.

Questions: Can you see the connection? How do you rely on God for the return in your children's lives?

Study Notes

_____

_____

_____

_____

_____

_____

_____

_____

Application: Not one of you as a parent woke up this morning with the intent to sow grief, discord, rebellion, or selfishness into your child. Instead, you protected, guided, nurtured, and selflessly gave yourself. It's not how you were reared or the atmosphere you grew up in as a child or young adult that determines how you will be as a parent. It may have had an influence on you, but when you surrendered and gave your life to the transformation of the Holy Spirit, how you think and make decisions now has changed. You are no longer bound to past influences. So, you choose. You choose how you will influence your children. Each day you try to show your children the importance of not walking in the mistakes you made. Or you encourage your children to follow the successes you have had. This is the best way, and this is why. There is no better teacher and example than a living experience. To the best of your abilities, you coach, teach, and model how to love the Lord and put Him first.

Teach your children how to make decisions, that their choices have consequences, and that they have to live through their choices. Do they choose to follow the ways of God? They alone are responsible for the consequences of their own decisions. As a parent, you need to be transparent enough to model wise choices in front of your children. They need to see you as real and trusting the Lord with all of your heart.

You should be a parent who demonstrates your love, devotion, and passion toward God in your everyday living before your children—with no strings attached or manipulative intent, just honest role modeling before your children. How your children perceive your actions will create either desire or rejection, but you're accountable only to walk out your love and passion for God, to teach His principles, and to stand for Him the best way you know how before them. Trust God for the results. You can't control the outcome. You can only trust that at the end of the day, you've done the best you could.

Further Study

Read 1 Chronicles 29:11-12; Proverbs 1:8, 20:20, 23:22, 30:17; Matthew 22:21; and Ephesians 6:1-3. I know you want to honor God's principles. Ask yourself if you need to change some of the behaviors that you are engaged in now. Authority—good, bad, or ugly—comes from God. Nothing escapes the notice of God. Your responsibility is to honor the promises and favor from God on your life.

NOTES

_____

_____

_____

_____

_____

_____

_____

_____

_____

_____

_____

_____

_____

"The Lord is a warrior..."
Exodus 15:3 (NET)

Part 1: The Warrior Covenant

Lesson 3
Our Covenant With Others

I will love and treat my neighbor the way I would like to be treated. Mark 12:31; Luke 6:27-42; Rom. 13:8-10; Gal. 5:13-15; James 2:8-9; 1 John 4:7-21

C. S. Lewis once said,

> To love at all is to be vulnerable. Love anything, and your heart will certainly be wrung and possibly be broken. If you want to make sure of keeping it intact, you must give your heart to no one, not even to an animal. Wrap it carefully round with hobbies and little luxuries; avoid all entanglements. Lock it up safe in the casket or coffin or your selfishness. But in that casket—safe, dark, motionless, airless—it will change. It will not be broken; it will become unbreakable, impenetrable, irredeemable...The only place outside of Heaven where you can be perfectly safe from all the dangers...of love is Hell.

To love or not to love, that is the question. Loving others is a messy business. You are at risk because you expose yourself to being vulnerable, but in doing so, there is great reward and joy. Thomas a' Kempis said it this way, "Whoever loves much, does much." Reach out and love others; Jesus would want you to.

DISCUSSION

Romans 13:8-10 (NKJV) says:

> *Owe no one anything except to love one another, for he who loves another has fulfilled the law. ⁹For the commandments, "You shall not commit adultery," "You shall not murder," "You shall not steal," "You shall not bear false witness," "You shall not covet," and if there is any other*

commandment, are all summed up in this saying, namely, "You shall love your neighbor as your-self." ¹⁰Love does no harm to a neighbor; therefore love is the fulfillment of the law.

1 John 4:7–21 (MEV) says:

Beloved, let us love one another, for love is of God, and everyone who loves is born of God and knows God. *⁸Anyone who does not love does not know God, for God is love. ⁹In this way the love of God was revealed to us, that God sent His only begotten Son into the world, that we might live through Him.* **¹⁰In this is love: not that we loved God, but that He loved us and sent His Son to be the atoning sacrifice for our sins.** *¹¹Beloved, if God so loved us, we must also love one an-other. ¹²No one has seen God at any time. If we love one another, God dwells in us, and His love is perfected in us. ¹³We know that we live in Him, and He in us, because He has given us His Spirit. ¹⁴And we have seen and testify that the Father sent the Son to be the Savior of the world. ¹⁵Whoever confesses that Jesus is the Son of God, God lives in him, and he in God. ¹⁶And we have come to know and to believe the love that God has for us.* **God is love. Whoever lives in love lives in God, and God in him.** *¹⁷In this way God's love is perfected in us, so that we may have boldness on the Day of Judgment, because as He is, so are we in this world. ¹⁸There is no fear in love, but perfect love casts out fear, because fear has to do with punishment. Whoever fears is not perfect in love. ¹⁹We love Him because He first loved us.* **²⁰If anyone says, "I love God," and hates his brother, he is a liar. For whoever does not love his brother whom he has seen, how can he love God whom he has not seen?** *²¹We have this commandment from Him: Whoever loves God must also love his brother* (Emphasis added).

Questions: What does it really mean to love your neighbor? Why should it matter how you treat your neighbor? Is it that hard to reach out and extend a hand to another and show them the love Jesus showed you? Think about what keeps you from reaching out. Do you want to change? Being like Jesus is remembering what He has done for you and expressing it in your actions towards oth-ers. Can you say you really know God?

Study Notes

_____

_____

_____

_____

_____

_____

DISCUSSION

Luke 6:27-42 (NKJV) says:

But I say to you who hear: Love your enemies, do good to those who hate you, [28]bless those who curse you, and pray for those who spitefully use you. [29]To him who strikes you on the one cheek, offer the other also. And from him who takes away your cloak, do not withhold your tunic either. [30]Give to everyone who asks of you. And from him who takes away your goods do not ask them back. [31]And just as you want men to do to you, you also do to them likewise. [32]But if you love those who love you, what credit is that to you? For even sinners love those who love them. [33]And if you do good to those who do good to you, what credit is that to you? For even sinners do the same. [34]And if you lend to those from whom you hope to receive back, what credit is that to you? For even sinners lend to sinners to receive as much back. [35]But love your enemies, do good, and lend, hoping for nothing in return; and your reward will be great, and you will be sons of the Most High. For He is kind to the unthankful and evil. [36]Therefore be merciful, just as your Father also is merciful. [37]"Judge not, and you shall not be judged. Condemn not, and you shall not be condemned. Forgive, and you will be forgiven. [38]Give, and it will be given to you: good measure, pressed down, shaken together, and running over will be put into your bosom. For with the same measure that you use, it will be measured back to you." [39]And He spoke a parable to them: Can the blind lead the blind? Will they not both fall into the ditch? [40]A disciple is not above his teacher, but everyone who is perfectly trained will be like his teacher. [41]And why do you look at the speck in your brother's eye, but do not perceive the plank in your own eye? [42]Or how can you say to your brother, 'Brother, let me remove the speck that is in your eye,' when you yourself do not see the plank that is in your own eye? Hypocrite! First remove the plank from your own eye, and then you will see clearly to remove the speck that is in your brother's eye.

Questions: What *love in action* can you see in this passage? Reflect and ask yourself how you should treat your neighbor. Why put yourself out there as a disciple of Jesus to be like the teacher and to love the way He loved others?

Study Notes

_____

_____

_____

_____

_____

Questions: *What about your attitude? Is your attitude reflected in your expression of love toward your neighbor? Why not just keep to yourself and not be bothered by anyone or bother anyone? Love is fulfilled through expression and demonstration. Practice small acts of kindness.* Little things add up to great love!

Study Notes

_____

_____

_____

_____

_____

_____

_____

_____

_____

DISCUSSION

John 15:1-5 (NASB77) says:

I am the true vine, and My Father is the vinedresser. ²Every branch in Me that does not bear fruit, He takes away; and every branch that bears fruit, He prunes it, that it may bear more fruit. ³You are already clean because of the word which I have spoken to you. ⁴Abide in Me, and I in you. As the branch cannot bear fruit of itself, unless it abides in the vine, so neither can you, unless you abide in Me. ⁵I am the vine, you are the branches; he who abides in Me, and I in him, he bears much fruit; for apart from Me you can do nothing.

Philippians 4:13 (NASB77) says:

I can do all things through Him who strengthens me.

Questions: What gives you the power or ability to love your neighbor? Love is action. In your own strength, you can do nothing that lasts, but through Christ who strengthens you, your life can be fruitful. What are some of the evidences of a fruitful life?

Study Notes

_____

_____

_____

_____

_____

_____

_____

_____

DISCUSSION

The "Golden Rule." You know it as "Do unto others as you would like for them to do unto you."

Matthew 7:12 (NASB77) says:

Therefore, however you want people to treat you, so treat them, for this is the Law and the Prophets.

Matthew 22:39 (NASB77) says:

'YOU SHALL LOVE YOUR NEIGHBOR AS YOURSELF.'

Questions: What act of sowing can you sow towards another that you would want to come back to you? The joy is in the giving; it's in releasing, not in tightly holding. Do you believe it is more blessed to give than to receive?

Study Notes

_____

_____

_____

_____

_____

Application: Who is your neighbor? Maybe it's the family or person next door, the individual asking for food that you pass when you are going to the mall, the person everyone talks about in a less than honorable way, or that person you work with every day that you just don't seem to connect with. What would Jesus do in any of these situations? What can you do? Sometimes it doesn't take much—an outstretched hand, an encouraging word, or just noticing they are there. You say, "Well that's Jesus; I'm not Jesus." I know, but the Holy Spirit is making you like Him. Every day you are becoming more like Him. His love, compassion, and mercy should flow through all of us. I understand you're busy. Life is pulling on you, and it's not easy. Neighbors are all around you, and your actions might just be the only Jesus they see today. We all need more of Him and less of our own will in our lives. Just take a little extra time to be alert for opportunities around you. Practice "What would Jesus do?" when it comes to that neighbor right next to you. There is no reward in grudgingly doing anything for the Lord. Our Father sees what we do in secret. He knows our hearts, our thoughts, even the very hairs on our head, and still He asks, "Will you love your neighbor just as my son Jesus loves you?"

Further Study

Deuteronomy 15:7-11	Leviticus 19:9-18	Proverbs 3:28, 29; 17:17; 27:10
Matthew 5:39-48	John 15:13	Romans 12:13, 14; 15:1, 2
Galatians 5:22-23; 6:10	Colossians 3:17, 23, 24	

You never know when you will be in need. It's valuable to have a neighbor nearby for your time of need. The way you treat others matters. How we live next to and around others plays a big part in our daily living. It's easy to cultivate neighborliness. Read the parable of the good Samaritan again, Luke 10:30-37. Ask yourself, "Who am I in this story? Would I stop or would I be in too much of a hurry? Would I give my resources?" I think you would! If you have surrounded yourself with neighbors into whose lives you have sown, then you will reap your response from that sowing when you are in need.

I will not allow my liberty or freedom in Christ to be a stumbling block to others, neither judging them nor causing others to fall away, lose faith, or blaspheme God because of my liberty. Rom. 14:12-23; 1 Cor. 8:4-13, 10:23-30; Gal. 5:13-14

1 Corinthians 6:12 (TLB) says:

> *I can do anything I want to if Christ has not said no, but some of these things aren't good for me. Even if I am allowed to do them, I'll refuse to if I think they might get such a grip on me that I can't easily stop when I want to.*

Thomas Huxley once said, "A man's worst difficulties begin when he is able to do as he likes." Left to ourselves, we want to be unchecked and unaccountable for any and all of our actions. However, yielding our self to the Holy Spirit of God produces restraint and consideration for others and influences how our actions are perceived by others.

DISCUSSION

1 Corinthians 8:4-13 (AMP) says:

> *In this matter, then, of eating food offered to idols, we know that an idol is nothing (has no real existence) and that there is no God but one. [5]For although there may be so-called gods, whether in heaven or on earth, as indeed there are many of them, both of gods and of lords and masters, [6]Yet for us there is [only] one God, the Father, Who is the Source of all things and for Whom we [have life], and one Lord, Jesus Christ, through and by Whom are all things and through and by Whom we [ourselves exist]. [7]Nevertheless, not all [believers] possess this knowledge. But some, through being all their lives until now accustomed to [thinking of] idols [as real and living], still consider the food [offered to an idol] as that sacrificed to an [actual] god; and their weak consciences become defiled and injured if they eat [it]. [8]Now food [itself] will not cause our acceptance by God nor commend us to Him. Eating [food offered to idols] gives us no advantage; neither do we come short or become any worse if we do not eat [it]. [9]Only be careful that this power of choice (this permission and liberty to do as you please) which is yours, does not [somehow] become a hindrance (cause of stumbling) to the weak or overscrupulous [giving them an impulse to sin]. [10]For suppose someone sees you, a man having knowledge [of God, with an intelligent view of this subject and] reclining at table in an idol's temple, might he not be encouraged and emboldened [to violate his own conscientious scruples] if he is weak and uncertain, and eat what [to him] is for the purpose of idol worship? [11]And so by your enlightenment (your knowledge of spiritual things), this weak man is ruined (is lost and perishes)—the brother for whom Christ (the Messiah) died! [12]And when you sin against your brethren in this way, wounding and damaging their weak conscience, you sin against Christ. [13]Therefore, if [my eating a] food is a*

cause of my brother's falling or of hindering [his spiritual advancement], I will not eat [such] flesh forever, lest I cause my brother to be tripped up and fall and to be offended.

1 Corinthians 10:13-30 (NASB77) says:

All things are lawful, but not all things are profitable. All things are lawful, but not all things edify. [24]*Let no one seek his own good, but that of his neighbor.* [25]*Eat anything that is sold in the meat market, without asking questions for conscience' sake;* [26]*FOR THE EARTH IS THE LORD'S, AND ALL IT CONTAINS.* [27]*If one of the unbelievers invites you, and you wish to go, eat anything that is set before you, without asking questions for conscience' sake.* [28]*But if anyone should say to you, "This is meat sacrificed to idols," do not eat it, for the sake of the one who informed you, and for conscience' sake;* [29]*I mean not your own conscience, but the other man's; for why is my freedom judged by another's conscience?* [30]*If I partake with thankfulness, why am I slandered concerning that for which I give thanks?*

Questions: In your own words, what would you say *liberty* means? Why should you be concerned about your actions or care if your decisions edify another or not? What limits your liberty?

Study Notes

_____

_____

_____

_____

Questions: What is a stumbling block? Can you give some examples of stumbling blocks? Are stumbling blocks any different from sins such as adultery? What part does the violation of another's conscience play in the exercise of my liberty? What constitutes a misuse of my liberty? After all, isn't it my liberty? Can't I do whatever I want as long as my conscience is not bothered?

Study Notes

_____

_____

_____

_____

Questions: Can your attitude toward liberty affect your becoming more like Jesus? Can it affect your growth in Christ or cause stagnation in your life? How?

Study Notes

_____

_____

_____

_____

_____

_____

Application: You are free in Christ and set free once you have accepted Christ into your life. No one can take away your liberty (freedom). Yes, you have liberty. Yes, you have freedom, but not all choices and actions are beneficial. If your choice hurts another Christian (maybe one who is less mature), it would be better to lay aside your liberty by choice because you don't want to cause hurt and confusion or wreck another person's faith in Christ. If Jesus told us to put others before ourselves, then in applying that to our liberty, we would lay aside our choice if it were detrimental to another.

Loving another person rather than blowing past them is acting like Jesus. You make daily decisions that reflect your heart, and you freely exercise your will. As you surrender to the will of God, you learn to yield your liberty in order to mirror and honor Jesus. Your actions either encourage others to or discourage others from following the principles of God. Believe it or not, others watch your life to see if you are real or fake—very much like Jim was watching me while I was deployed in Iraq. It does matter how we walk out our daily lives. People all around us are looking for real people who walk the walk. Your personal liberty allows you to do all things, yet not all things are profitable to a life dedicated to reflecting the life lived by Jesus. Real love restrains us from causing another to waver or trip up in their walk to be like God. Stumbling blocks cause others to trip up! Pride, a lack of humility, or even thoughtlessness towards others greatly impacts your individual walk before the Lord. Liberty requires you to exercise a great deal of seeking the good of others before seeking your own good. Where there is great freedom of choice, there is also a great responsibility to walk humbly before God. Live in peace and always put others first.

Further Study

Titus 2:11-14; 1 Peter 2:16; 1 John 2:15; Matthew 18:5-7; 1 Corinthians 6:12, 9:19; 1 Peter 2:16. A believer should not hide behind his liberty to indulge in wrong behavior.

I will be accountable to other men, to my wife and to my family. Prov. 13:20, 17:17, 18:1, 27:17; Gal. 5:15-21, 6:1-5; 1 Thess. 5:11-15; Heb. 10:24-25; James 5:16

John Wesley sometimes had the members of his congregation ask each other the following questions:

1. Have you been with a woman anywhere this past week that might be seen as compromising?
2. Have any of your financial dealings lacked integrity?
3. Have you exposed yourself to any sexually explicit material?
4. Have you spent adequate time in Bible study and prayer?
5. Have you given priority time to your family?
6. Have you fulfilled the mandates of your calling?
7. Have you just lied to me?

Some might think, *I don't need to answer any of these questions,* and to that, I would say *You're right, but why wouldn't you?* Our lives are sending a message to others around us. Every day you are being watched by someone. Daniel Webster once said, "My greatest thought is my accountability to God." Economist Sir Josiah Stamp once said, "It is easy to dodge our responsibilities, but we cannot dodge the consequences of dodging our responsibilities."

Let **1 Corinthians 10:13** (TLB) guide and strengthen you:

But remember this—the wrong desires that come into your life aren't anything new and different. Many others have faced exactly the same problems before you. And no temptation is irresistible. You can trust God to keep the temptation from becoming so strong that you can't stand up against it, for he has promised this and will do what he says. He will show you how to escape temptation's power so that you can bear up patiently against it.

Question: What is the definition of *accountability* in your own words?

DISCUSSION

Proverbs 27:17 (NKJV) says:

As iron sharpens iron, so a man sharpens the countenance of his friend.

Questions: How do we sharpen each other? Are you your "brother's keeper"? If so, how; if not, why not?

Study Notes

_____

_____

_____

_____

_____

_____

_____

Questions: What are some of the benefits of being in relationships with and accountable to other believers?

Study Notes

_____

_____

_____

_____

_____

_____

_____

DISCUSSION

James 5:16 (MEV) says:

> *Confess your faults to one another and pray for one another, that you may be healed. The effective, fervent prayer of a righteous man accomplishes much.*

Questions: What should you confess to each other? Shouldn't confession of certain sins be reserved for conversations with God?

Study Notes

_____

_____

_____

_____

_____

_____

_____

_____

DISCUSSION

Galatians 5:15-25 (NKJV) says:

But if you bite and devour one another, beware lest you be consumed by one another! [16]*I say then: Walk in the Spirit, and you shall not fulfill the lust of the flesh.* [17]*For the flesh lusts against the Spirit, and the Spirit against the flesh; and these are contrary to one another, so that you do not do the things that you wish.* [18]*But if you are led by the Spirit, you are not under the law.* [19]*Now the works of the flesh are evident, which are: adultery, fornication, uncleanness, lewdness,* [20]*idolatry, sorcery, hatred, contentions, jealousies, outbursts of wrath, selfish ambitions, dissensions, heresies,* [21]*envy, murders, drunkenness, revelries, and the like; of which I tell you beforehand, just as I also told you in time past, that those who practice such things will not inherit the kingdom of God.* [22]*But the fruit of the Spirit is love, joy, peace, longsuffering, kindness, goodness, faithfulness,* [23]*gentleness, self-control. Against such there is no law.* [24]*And those who are Christ's have crucified the flesh with its passions and desires. If we live in the Spirit, let us also walk in the Spirit.*

Galatians 6:1-5 (NASB77) says:

Brethren, even if a man is caught in any trespass, you who are spiritual, restore such a one in a spirit of gentleness; **each one** *looking to yourself, lest you too be tempted.* [2]*Bear one another's burdens, and thus fulfill the law of Christ.* [3]*For if anyone thinks he is something when he is nothing, he deceives himself.* [4]*But let each one examine his own work, and then he will have* **reason** *for boasting in regard to himself alone, and not in regard to another.* [5]*For each one shall bear his own load* (Emphasis added).

Hebrews 10:24, 25 (NKJV) says:

And let us consider one another in order to stir up love and good works, ²⁵not forsaking the assembling of ourselves together, as is the manner of some, but exhorting one another, and so much the more as you see the Day approaching.

Questions: What admonitions do these verses give you about how to treat one another or care for your fellow Christian? What role do you play in looking out for and holding accountable your brother in the Lord? What are some examples of things you have done to encourage your brothers in the Lord? Have you ever had to restore someone? How did you do it? What does the Galatians 6 passage say you should watch out for?

Study Notes

_____

_____

_____

_____

_____

_____

_____

Application: None of us is without fault. We all come short, but God gives us fellow Christians to help us face the daily pressures of life. None of us is an island, so we need to reach out and share a hand or a listening ear. Two (or more) are better than one. Ask yourself, "How can I today reach out to another?"

Each of us has a responsibility to be accountable for not just our material wealth, but for our actions, thoughts, talents, and life choices. Being accountable means being answerable for our actions and willingly submitting to another voluntarily. Those who offer to help should not lord over another or bully another but should be humble. Stepping up to take responsibility for other people in your life can be challenging but extremely fulfilling as you allow yourself to be led and used by the Holy Spirit and the Word of God. Really caring for and wanting to walk alongside of others can be messy. Know that what God calls you to do, He will also empower and equip you to do. His strength and ability are what matters, not yours.

Further Study

Ecclesiastes 4:9-12	Jeremiah 17:9-10	Ezekiel 18:19, 20
Matthew 7:3-5; 12:33-37	Luke 12:35-48; 16:10-12	Romans 6:1, 2; 12:9-13; 14:7-12
1 Corinthians 3:10-15, 4:1, 2	Colossians 3:12-17	Hebrews 4:11-13; 10:24-25; 12:9
Hebrews 13:1-3, 17	1 Peter 4:7-11; 5:1-5	I John 1:5-10

Notes:

"The LORD is a warrior..."
Exodus 15:3 (NET)

Part 1: The Warrior Covenant

Lesson 4
Our Covenant With Self

I will seek knowledge, wisdom, discernment, and understanding. 1 Kings 3:6-9, 12; Prov. 2:1-8, 3:13, 4:20-22, 19:20; Matt. 7:7-8; James 1:5-6

The story has been told of a dispassionate young man who once approached the Greek philosopher Socrates and casually said, "O great Socrates, I come to you for knowledge." The philosopher took the young man down to the sea, waded in with him, and then dunked him under the water for thirty seconds. When he let the young man up for air, Socrates asked him to repeat what he wanted. "Knowledge, O great one," he sputtered.

Socrates put him under the water again, only this time a little longer. After several repeated dunkings and responses, the philosopher asked, "What do you want?"

The young man finally gasped, "Air. I want air!"

"Good," answered Socrates. "Now, when you want knowledge as much as you wanted air, you shall have it."

Do you have that passion for knowledge and wisdom? Notice the following quotes concerning wisdom: "A wise man learns from the mistakes of others. Nobody lives long enough to make them all himself"; "A wise man learns by the experience of others. An ordinary man learns by his own experience. A fool learns by nobody's experience"; "Experience is learning from your mistakes. Wisdom is learning from others mistakes."

DISCUSSION

1 Kings 3:3-9 (MEV) says:

Solomon loved the LORD, walking in the statutes of his father David, though he sacrificed and burned incense at the high places. ⁴The king went to Gibeon to sacrifice there, for that was the great high place, and he offered a thousand burnt offerings on that altar. ⁵While he was in Gibeon, the LORD appeared to Solomon in a dream at night, and He said, "Ask what you want from Me." ⁶Solomon answered, "You have shown great mercy to your servant David my father, because he walked before You in faithfulness, righteousness, and uprightness of heart toward You. And You have shown him great kindness in giving him a son to sit on his throne this day. ⁷"Now, O LORD, my God, You have made Your servant king in place of my father David, and I am still a little child and do not know how to go out or come in. ⁸And Your servant is in the midst of Your people whom You have chosen, a great people, so numerous that they cannot be numbered or counted. ⁹Give Your servant therefore an understanding heart to judge Your people, that I may discern between good and bad, for who is able to judge among so great a people?"

Questions: How was David described by his son Solomon? Do you think Solomon was awed by the shadow of his father David? What was Solomon asking for from God? Why do you think his prayer was granted? Describe Solomon's attitude while making his request before God. Why was God pleased with Solomon's question?

Study Notes

_____

_____

_____

_____

_____

_____

_____

_____

DISCUSSION

Proverbs 2:1-8 (NKJV) says:

My son, if you receive my words, And treasure my commands within you, ²So that you incline your ear to wisdom, And apply your heart to understanding; ³Yes, if you cry out for discernment, And lift up your voice for understanding, ⁴If you seek her as silver, And search for her as for hidden treasures; ⁵Then you will understand the fear of the LORD, And find the knowledge of God. ⁶For the LORD gives wisdom; From His mouth come knowledge and understanding; ⁷He stores up sound wisdom for the upright; He is a shield to those who walk uprightly; ⁸He guards the paths of justice, And preserves the way of His saints.

Questions: In your own words, describe wisdom, discernment, and understanding? How should you value and seek for wisdom, discernment, and understanding? What is your responsibility in your walk, your daily living, before God? What do you hope to gain from your pursuit? In Solomon's proverb, can you sense the passion in these verses?

Study Notes

_____

_____

_____

_____

_____

Application: Is Solomon's request any different from one you can make today to God? Do you need wisdom for your day-to-day living? God is still challenging diligent, passionate seekers to take hold of His promises for their life. How desperately do you want them? Are there circumstances in your life in which discernment and keenly selective judgment might be beneficial? What are some things you are facing for which you need understanding?

As you face difficult parental decisions, work choices, or a life-changing course that will shape your present for many years to come, God wants to give you guidance and to ease your burden if you will turn to Him for help. Passion for God produces an audience with God, which results in action by God.

Further Study:

Exodus 31:1-5; 36:1;	1 Samuel 2:3	2 Chronicles 1:12
Psalms 26:3; 51:6; 86:11,	Psalms 94:10; 119:1, 66	Proverbs 1:4, 2:1-22 (TLB or AMP)
Proverbs10:9; 15:21	Proverbs 22:12; 28:26	Ecclesiastes 2:26
Isaiah 28:9; 33:6	Jeremiah 24:7; 31:34	Daniel 1:17; 2:21
Hosea 14:9	Matthew 11:25;13:11;	John 3:21
Acts 6:8-10	1 Corinthians 1:5, 2:12, 12:8	2 Corinthians 4:6
Ephesians 1:17	James 1:17	2 John 1:6

Colossians 2:3 (*cf.* Exodus 8:10, Psalm 73:11, Jeremiah 3:15, John 3:27)

I will put off completely my selfish, sinful life, put on the new life found in Christ Jesus, and submit to the renewing of my mind that He might sanctify me, having cleansed me by the washing of water with the Word. Rom. 12:1-2; 2 Cor. 5:17-19; Eph. 4:22-24; Phil. 4:8-9; Col. 3:8-17; James 1:21

Putting the past behind you is sometimes more difficult to practice than you might realize. Moving ahead to live the life God intends for us often involves separating ourselves from others around us. Athanasius, early bishop of Alexandria, found himself in that very situation. He stoutly opposed the teachings of Arius, who declared that Christ was not the eternal Son of God, but a subordinate being.

Hounded through five exiles, Athanasius was finally summoned before emperor Theodosius, who demanded he cease his opposition to Arius. The emperor reproved him and asked, "Do you not realize that all the world is against you?"

Athanasius quickly answered, "Then I am against all the world."

Christ lived differently than those around Him. You too will have to move ahead and allow your life to be transformed. Pastor, Dr. Warren W. Wiersbe once said, "Do not say, 'Why were the former days better than these?' You do not move ahead by constantly looking in a rear view mirror. The past is a rudder to guide you, not an anchor to drag you. We must learn from the past but not live in the past." Let's continue to move ahead together.

DISCUSSION

Romans 12:1, 2 (NKJV) says:

> *I beseech you therefore, brethren, by the mercies of God, that you present your bodies a living sacrifice, holy, acceptable to God, which is your reasonable service. ²And do not be conformed to this world, but be transformed by the renewing of your mind, that you may prove what is that good and acceptable and perfect will of God.*

Questions: Why should you heed Paul's warning not to conform to this world? What is he referring to in this passage? In your own words, what does it mean to conform? The opposite of conformity is rebellion or non-compliance. How should you present yourself and describe what that looks like to you?

Study Notes

_____

_____

_____

_____

_____

_____

_____

DISCUSSION

Ephesians 4:17-24 (NIV) says:

> So I tell you this, and insist on it in the Lord, that you must no longer live as the Gentiles do, in the futility of their thinking. [18]They are darkened in their understanding and separated from the life of God because of the ignorance that is in them due to the hardening of their hearts. [19]Having lost all sensitivity, they have given themselves over to sensuality so as to indulge in every kind of impurity, with a continual lust for more. [20]You, however, did not come to know Christ that way. [21]Surely you heard of him and were taught in him in accordance with the truth that is in Jesus. **[22]You were taught, with regard to your former way of life, to put off your old self, which is being corrupted by its deceitful desires; [23]to be made new in the attitude of your minds; [24]and to put on the new self, created to be like God in true righteousness and holiness** (Emphasis added).

Questions: Explain, in your own words, what is meant by deceitful desires. Why do you think it is so difficult for people to walk away from their present/former lifestyle choices for ones that are completely uncertain? Was it difficult for you to walk away? What do you think needs to happen before a person desires a change in his life? Why do you think it is so hard to change? What does it mean to put off something? How do you renew your mind?

Study Notes

_____

_____

_____

_____

_____

_____

_____

_____

DISCUSSION

Colossians 3:8-17 (NKJV) says:

> But now you yourselves are to **put off all these**: anger, wrath, malice, blasphemy, filthy language out of your mouth. ⁹Do not lie to one another, since you have **put off** the old man with his deeds, ¹⁰and have **put on** the new man who is renewed in knowledge according to the image of Him who created him, ¹¹where there is neither Greek nor Jew, circumcised nor uncircumcised, barbarian, Scythian, slave nor free, but Christ is all and in all. ¹²Therefore, as the elect of God, holy and beloved, **put on** tender mercies, kindness, humility, meekness, longsuffering; ¹³bearing with one another, and forgiving one another, if anyone has a complaint against another; even as Christ forgave you, so you also must do. ¹⁴But above all these things **put on** love, which is the bond of perfection. ¹⁵And let the peace of God rule in your hearts, to which also you were called in one body; and be thankful. ¹⁶Let the word of Christ dwell in you richly in all wisdom, teaching and admonishing one another in psalms and hymns and spiritual songs, singing with grace in your hearts to the Lord. ¹⁷And **whatever you do in word or deed, do all in the name of the Lord Jesus, giving thanks to God the Father through Him** (Emphasis added).

Questions: How easy is it for you to "put off," lay aside, or cast off the things described in this passage? Do you want to share any of your struggles? Can you make a change in your own strength? Why not? What characteristics are we laying aside, and what qualities are we substituting? What part does the action of loving play in our transformation?

Study Notes

_____

_____

_____

_____

_____

_____

_____

Application: Renewing your heart, mind, and soul is not an easy thing to do; it is impossible to do in your own effort. Your former lifestyle was interwoven with habits and choices that have become comfortable and pleasurable to you, and before you realized the need for change by and through the Holy Spirit, you were duped into thinking you were okay. That, my friend, is the deceitfulness of sin and your former conduct. If you have soiled, dirty clothes, you put them into the washing machine with soap to clean them. After the process of washing, the clothes are renewed and clean. There is action involved on the part of the one wanting or needing renewal; it just doesn't happen on its own.

Unless you take the first step, there is no chance for change. Envision yourself taking off your present life, exchanging it for a new life, and putting on the life God wants for you. The renewing of your mind involves taking on new attitudes and ideas. Your growth as a Christian is a process of daily choices to move you continuously toward being more like Jesus by imitating Him; you do that by surrendering your will to the will of God for your life. Where do you want to be? Changing wrong habits and putting on godly character is a process, and it does not happen overnight. Persistence and patiently submitting yourself to the transforming process of God make all change possible. Do others see someone who has been changed? It's only by God's grace, mercy, and the sacrifice of Jesus that we can be renewed. Your own strength and effort cannot produce lasting results, but your renewed mind and spirit come through God.

"Never be afraid to trust an unknown future to a known God." – Corrie Ten Boom

Further Study

Psalms 51:2-12; 69:5   Ezekiel 36:26   Romans 6:6; 8:9; 13:13-14
Galatians 5:16-26   Ephesians 2:8-10   Titus 3:5

I will, by God's grace, commit to being patient and kind; not jealous, boastful, proud or rude; not demanding my own way; not irritable or keeping records of wrong; not taking part in injustice; not being self-willed, quick-tempered, or violent; not be greedy but hospitable, sober minded, just, and self controlled." 1 Cor. 13:4-7; Gal. 5:22-26, 1 Tim. 3:8-13; Titus 1:5-9

You might be familiar with the traditional adage, "Sow a thought, reap an act; sow an act, reap a habit; sow a habit, reap a character; sow a character, reap a destiny." Add to these words what former coach John Wooden of the UCLA Bruins basketball team said, "Be more concerned with your character than with your reputation. Your character is what you really are, while your reputation is merely what others think you are." Coach Wooden also said, "The true test of a man's character is what he does when no one is watching," and "Happiness begins where selfishness ends." Developing the character of Christ takes time and a redirecting of our focus from our self to others. Let's continue to develop the character of Christ in our lives.

DISCUSSION

1 Corinthians 13:4-7 (TLB) says:

> *Love is very patient and kind, never jealous or envious, never boastful or proud, ⁵never haughty or selfish or rude. Love does not demand its own way. It is not irritable or touchy. It does not hold grudges and will hardly even notice when others do it wrong. ⁶It is never glad about injustice, but rejoices whenever truth wins out. ⁷If you love someone, you will be loyal to him no matter what the cost. You will always believe in him, always expect the best of him, and always stand your ground in defending him.*

Questions: This is an amazing passage, packed full of challenge. How can you exhibit these qualities of love in your daily life? Is there any one quality that stands out to you more than other qualities? Why is it so hard to incorporate these qualities into our lives? Do you think your priorities need to change at all? If so, how?

Study Notes

_____

_____

_____

_____

_____
_____
_____
_____

DISCUSSION

Galatians 5:22-26 (NKJV)

But the fruit of the Spirit is love, joy, peace, longsuffering, kindness, goodness, faithfulness, [23]gentleness, self-control. Against such there is no law. [24]And those who are Christ's have crucified the flesh with its passions and desires. [25]If we live in the Spirit, let us also walk in the Spirit. [26]Let us not become conceited, provoking one another, envying one another.

Questions: In these verses, we find a lot to chew on. Stop and ask yourself, "Would others describe my life with these attributes?" What fruit do you identify with most? Which ones are most challenging? How do you treat others? Would you consider yourself others-focused?

Study Notes

_____
_____
_____
_____
_____
_____
_____

"The best index to a person's character is (a) how he treats people who can't do him any good, and (b) how he treats people who can't fight back." –Abigail Van Buren

Application: Life is character; you either have character or you don't. Always remember that the oak tree didn't grow strong and tall overnight, but time, adversity, and watering developed the great oak. Our lives are no different. Jesus invested His life in you so that you can be a different man. Be real with yourself and transparent with others. Don't say, "I may as well give up now." No, live your life one step at a time, and one day at a time. Yield yourself to the transformative influence of the Holy Spirit. Change is possible, but only through the grace and mercy of God.

There will be days when you reflect and think you are doing great and growing. Then the next day it may seem like you are falling apart, losing ground and hope. Stand your ground and fight; then expect and anticipate the Holy Spirit's empowerment. When you surrender to the Master's molding and shaping of your life, the Refiner's fire works out the impurities in your character. Your circumstances test and reflect your true nature. You do not have a choice about growing; you must grow. You do not have a choice concerning struggles; struggles will come in order to grow.

Life is a struggle; otherwise, you would be living in a false reality. The victory comes because you do not have to do anything on your own. God helps you during your struggles. Your character then develops and becomes more like Jesus' character. Time produces fruit, or growth, in your life. As you look at your life, you may not recognize that your character is now different, but others will see change in you. Where you are at today is not where you will be tomorrow or the next day! Be encouraged. We are all in this together, and you are not alone.

Further Study

Proverbs 14:15	John 13:34-35	Romans 12:10
Ephesians 4:32	Philippians 2:3, 2:1-15	1 Peter 4:8

I will daily live by the Word of God through the power of the Holy Spirit. Ps. 19:7-14, 111:10, 119:2, 11, 97-98, 105, 130; Matt. 4:4; 2 Tim. 3:16-17; Heb. 4:12-13

Bible readers have sometimes been compared to a butterfly or a bee.

One is remarkable for its imposing plumage, which shows in the sunbeams like the dust of gems; as you watch its jaunty gyrations over the fields and its minuet dance from flower to flower, you cannot help admiring its graceful activity, for it is plainly getting over a great deal of ground. But in the same field there is another worker, whose brown vest and businesslike, straightforward flight may not have arrested your eye. His fluttering neighbor darts down here and there and sips elegantly wherever he can find a drop of ready nectar; but this dingy plodder makes a point of alighting everywhere, and wherever he alights he either finds honey or makes it. If the flower-cup be deep, he goes down to the bottom; if its dragon-mouth be shut, he thrusts its lips asunder; and if the nectar be peculiar, he explores all about till he discovers it....His rival of the painted velvet wing has no patience for such dull and long-winded details....The one died last October. The other is warm in his hive, amidst the fragrant stores he has gathered.

Now let me ask you this question: do you approach reading the Word of God like the butterfly or the bee?

You might say, I read the Bible when I can, because my schedule keeps me from being able to spend very much time reading the Bible. Consider the life and example of George Müller, a Christian evangelist and director of the Ashley Down Orphanage in Bristol, England, who died at the age of 92 in 1898 after caring for 10,024 orphans in his lifetime and establishing 117 schools that offered Christian education to over 120,000 children, many of them orphans. After having read the Bible through one hundred times with increasing delight, Müller made this statement:

I look upon it as a lost day when I have not had a good time over the Word of God. Friends often say, 'I have so much to do, so many people to see, I cannot find time for Scripture study.' Perhaps there are not many who have more to do than I. For more than half a century, I have never known one day when I had not more business than I could get through. For four years, I have had annually about 30,000 letters, and most of these have passed through my own hands. Then, as pastor of a church with 1,200 believers, great has been my care. Besides, I have had charge of five immense orphanages; also, at my publishing depot, the printing and circulating of millions of tracts, books, and Bibles; but I have always made it a rule never to begin work until I have had a good season with God and His Word. The blessing I have received has been wonderful.

DISCUSSION

Psalm 19:7-14 (NKJV) says:

The law of the LORD is perfect, converting the soul; The testimony of the LORD is sure, making wise the simple; ⁸The statutes of the LORD are right, rejoicing the heart; The commandment of the LORD is pure, enlightening the eyes; ⁹The fear of the LORD is clean, enduring forever; The judgments of the LORD are true and righteous altogether. ¹⁰More to be desired are they than gold, Yea, than much fine gold; Sweeter also than honey and the honeycomb. ¹¹Moreover by them Your servant is warned, And in keeping them there is great reward. ¹²Who can understand his errors? Cleanse me from secret faults. ¹³Keep back Your servant also from presumptuous sins; Let them not have dominion over me. Then I shall be blameless, And I shall be innocent of great transgression. ¹⁴Let the words of my mouth and the meditation of my heart Be acceptable in Your sight, O LORD, my strength and my Redeemer.

Psalm 111:10 (NKJV) says:

The fear of the LORD is the beginning of wisdom; A good understanding have all those who do His commandments. His praise endures forever.

Psalm 119:2 (MEV) says:

Blessed are those who keep His testimonies, and who seek Him with all their heart.

Psalm 119:11 (NKJV) says:

Your word I have hidden in my heart, That I might not sin against You!

Psalm 119:97, 98 (NKJV) says:

Oh, how I love Your law! It is my meditation all the day. You, through Your commandments, make me wiser than my enemies; For they are ever with me.

Psalm 119:105 (NKJV) says:

Your word is a lamp to my feet and a light to my path.

Psalm 119:130 (NKJV) says:

The entrance of Your words gives light; It gives understanding to the simple.

Questions: What do these verses say about the Word of God? Can you make a list of the attributes and benefits and how they might impact you? Do you want to be filled with wisdom, refreshed in your soul, warned of dangers, and protected from presumptuous sins? These are all benefits that come as you prioritize the Word of God in your life.

Study Notes

_____

_____

_____

_____

_____

_____

_____

_____

_____

DISCUSSION

Matthew 4:4 (TLB) says:

> *But Jesus told him, "No! For the Scriptures tell us that bread won't feed men's souls: obedience to every word of God is what we need."*

2 Timothy 3:16, 17 (TLB) says:

> *The whole Bible was given to us by inspiration from God and is useful to teach us what is true and to make us realize what is wrong in our lives; it straightens us out and helps us do what is right. [17]It is God's way of making us well prepared at every point, fully equipped to do good to everyone.*

2 Timothy 3:16, 17 (MEV) says:

> *All Scripture is inspired by God and is profitable for teaching, for reproof, for correction, and for instruction in righteousness, [17]that the man of God may be complete, thoroughly equipped for every good work.*

Questions: How much do you value the Word of God? Is there a difference between knowing and obeying a verse of Scripture? If so, what is it? What does "profitable for doctrine" mean to you? Do you see or believe that the Scriptures have the answers for all of your life's questions? Can you share some examples of how the Scriptures have helped you with a difficult decision or circumstance in your life?

Study Notes

_____

_____

_____

_____

_____

_____

_____

Questions: What does "the power of the Holy Spirit" mean to you? Asked another way, what does "being filled with the Holy Spirit" mean to you? What part does the Holy Spirit have in your daily life? How do you listen to the Holy Spirit as you read and study the scriptures?

Study Notes

_____

_____

_____

_____

_____

_____

_____

Point: The divinely breathed Word of God is extremely advantageous in the function of imparting instruction and providing evidence or proof as to why we need to correct our character or actions.

The Word of God fully equips the person who applies it to his life. He will lack nothing to complete the tasks set before him. The Word penetrates our heart, mind, and soul. It is able to discern or discriminate our thoughts and the intent of our lives.

Application: The astonishing thing about living the Christian life is that you do not have to do it on your own or by your own strength. The Holy Spirit will help you if you ask for and accept the help. You must desire help and direction from the Holy Spirit. Having a sense of being alive is found in the daily living and application of the Word of God. Is there a longing inside of you that says, "Yes, Lord, I want to follow your direction found in the Word of God, because it is the truth; I do not want to follow false or misguided philosophy"? Let the Scriptures change your life and your life choices. Very few days pass in your life where you do not feed your body and give it nutrition. In a similar way, you have to feed your spiritual life daily through taking in the Scriptures and communing in prayer, which is talking with God, often inspired by the Holy Spirit. This spiritual food prepares you for the daily challenges that you will face, equipping you and making you ready to face your circumstances.

No soldier in any army would ever think of going into combat without carrying his weapon or weapons of self-defense. Likewise, the Word of God acts as your spiritual weapon. It is your first line of defense against the Enemy of your physical and spiritual life. If you are weak in your knowledge and understanding of the Word of God, your Enemy will find that weakness and aggravate that vulnerability. The Holy Spirit's dynamic power in your life makes a difference. The Holy Spirit is your helper when you are in spiritual battle.

Further Study

Deuteronomy 8:3	Leviticus 18:5	Psalms 1:1-3; 107:9
Jeremiah 17:7, 8	Matthew 5:6	John 4:32-34, 6:48-63
Acts 17:10, 11	Ephesians 4:14	1 Thessalonians 2:13
Hebrews 13:9	1 Peter 2:2	2 Peter 1:20, 21

I will listen to and seek counsel from the Holy Spirit. 1 Chr. 28:8-9; Prov. 8:1-19; Luke 2:25-27a, 4:1, 11:9-13; Rom. 8:26-27; 1 John 2:27, 5:14

The following group of Scriptures tells both the importance and value of seeking counsel from the Holy Spirit. You will never go wrong listening to the voice of God.

Blessed [happy, fortunate, prosperous, and enviable] is the man who walks and lives not in the counsel of the ungodly [following their advice, their plans and purposes], nor stands [submissive and inactive] in the path where sinners walk, nor sits down [to relax and rest] where the scornful [and the mockers] gather (**Psalm 1:1** AMP).

Do not resentfully envy and be jealous of an unscrupulous, grasping man, and choose none of his ways. For the perverse are an abomination [extremely disgusting and detestable] to the Lord; but His confidential communion and secret counsel are with the [uncompromisingly] righteous (those who are upright and in right standing with Him) (**Proverbs 3:31-32** AMP).

The way of a fool is right in his own eyes, And whoso is hearkening to counsel is wise (**Proverbs 12:15** YLT).

But [only] with [God] are [perfect] wisdom and might; He [alone] has [true] counsel and understanding (**Job 12:13** AMP).

For if you live according to [the dictates of] the flesh, you will surely die. But if through the power of the [Holy] Spirit you are [habitually] putting to death (making extinct, deadening) the [evil] deeds prompted by the body, you shall [really and genuinely] live forever (**Romans 8:13** AMP).

But the Comforter (Counselor, Helper, Intercessor, Advocate, Strengthener, Standby), the Holy Spirit, Whom the Father will send in My name [in My place, to represent Me and act on My behalf], He will teach you all things. And He will cause you to recall (will remind you of, bring to your remembrance) everything I have told you (**John 14:26** AMP).

DISCUSSION

1 Chronicles 28:8, 9 (MEV) says:

Now therefore in the sight of all Israel, the assembly of the LORD, and in the hearing of our God, observe and seek out all the commandments of the LORD your God, that you may possess this good land and leave it for an inheritance for your children after you forever. ⁹As for you, Solomon my son, know the God of your fathers and serve Him with a whole heart and with a willing spirit, for the LORD searches every heart and understands the intent of every thought. If you seek Him, He will be found by you, but if you forsake Him, He will abandon you forever.

Proverbs 8:1-19 (TLB) says:

Can't you hear the voice of wisdom? She is standing at the city gates and at every fork in the road, and at the door of every house. Listen to what she says: ⁴⁻⁵*"Listen, men!" she calls. How foolish and naive you are! Let me give you understanding. O foolish ones, let me show you common sense!* ⁶⁻⁷*Listen to me! For I have important information for you. Everything I say is right and true, for I hate lies and every kind of deception.* ⁸*My advice is wholesome and good. There is nothing of evil in it.* ⁹*My words are plain and clear to anyone with half a mind—if it is only open!* ¹⁰*My instruction is far more valuable than silver or gold."*

¹¹For the value of wisdom is far above rubies; nothing can be compared with it. ¹²Wisdom and good judgment live together, for wisdom knows where to discover knowledge and understanding. ¹³If anyone respects and fears God, he will hate evil. For wisdom hates pride, arrogance, corruption, and deceit of every kind.

¹⁴⁻¹⁶I, Wisdom, give good advice and common sense. Because of my strength, kings reign in power, and rulers make just laws. ¹⁷I love all who love me. Those who search for me shall surely find me. ¹⁸Unending riches, honor, justice, and righteousness are mine to distribute. ¹⁹My gifts are better than the purest gold or sterling silver!

Questions: Look at the Chronicles passage and pay attention especially to verse 9. How should you serve God? According to this passage, what does God search? How does God look at your thoughts? Is there a difference in how we look for God? As you read the Proverbs passage, what do you find that wisdom can do for you? What attribute jumps out at you? Describe in your own words what diligently seeking God means.

Study Notes

_____

_____

_____

_____

_____

_____

DISCUSSION

Luke 11:9-13 (TLB) says:

And so it is with prayer—keep on asking and you will keep on getting; keep on looking and you will keep on finding; knock and the door will be opened. [10]Everyone who asks, receives; all who seek, find; and the door is opened to everyone who knocks. [11]You men who are fathers—if your boy asks for bread, do you give him a stone? If he asks for fish, do you give him a snake? [12]If he asks for an egg, do you give him a scorpion? [Of course not!] [13]"And if even sinful persons like yourselves give children what they need, don't you realize that your heavenly Father will do at least as much, and give the Holy Spirit to those who ask for him?"

Questions: What is your attitude when you ask or seek for anything from God? Does your attitude matter? If so, why? Are you daily asking for the Holy Spirit to give you guidance and wisdom? Give some examples of how the Holy Spirit has helped you. Do you quiet yourself before the Holy Spirit and listen? How do you prepare yourself to listen to God?

Study Notes

_____

_____

_____

_____

_____

_____

_____

Questions: *Asking, seeking,* and *knocking* are all verbs, they are action words, prompting you to engage and go after God. What do these words mean to you? What do the words *boldly pursuing God* suggest to you? We all have an advocate and a helper because of our relationship with the Holy Spirit. What does it mean to you to have the very Holy Spirit of God making intercession for you? Think about this point for a moment. The Holy Spirit knows the plan for your life, and He intercedes for you. How does that make you feel?

Study Notes

_____

_____

_____

_____

_____

_____

_____

_____

DISCUSSION

1 John 2:27 (TLB) says:

> But you have received the Holy Spirit, and he lives within you, in your hearts, so that you don't need anyone to teach you what is right. For he teaches you all things, and he is the Truth, and no liar; and so, just as he has said, you must live in Christ, never to depart from him.

1 John 5:14 (NKJV) says:

> Now this is the confidence that we have in Him, that if we ask anything according to His will, He hears us.

Romans 8:26, 27 (NKJV) says:

> Likewise the Spirit also helps in our weaknesses. For we do not know what we should pray for as we ought, but the Spirit Himself makes intercession for us with groanings which cannot be uttered. [27] Now He who searches the hearts knows what the mind of the Spirit is, because He makes intercession for the saints according to the will of God.

Questions: What is the confidence you can have? How do you explain the verses that say, "You do not need that anyone teach you"?

Study Notes

_____

_____

_____

_____

_____

_____

_____

Application: Every day you have needs in your life. Ask, seek, and knock at the door of the Holy Spirit to help you through your day. The Holy Spirit wants to be a part of your life, providing you with wisdom, guidance, and discernment for the decisions you face. Our Heavenly Father knows how to give good gifts, and He wants you to turn to Him first for all your concerns. The Holy Spirit is your guide. Will you let Him help you? You do not have to walk alone; you can be comforted, and you will be encouraged. Rely on the promptings of the Holy Spirit of God in your life. The Holy Spirit tarries and lingers with you to keep you from being deceived and led to believe that you don't understand how to walk before God. It's not that you should stop listening to others, but you should realize that if you are sincerely daily living a surrendered life before God, His promptings within you should not be discounted. These promptings serve as both warnings and confirmations. Walk in wisdom and walk closely each day with the Holy Spirit of God.

Further Study

Suggested Reading – *The Helper* by Catherine Marshall

Ask: Psalms 20:1, 37:4, 50:15, 91:5, 102:17; Proverbs 10:24, 15:8; Jeremiah 33:3; Matthew 6:6, 7:7-8, 21:22; Luke 18:7; John 14:13-14, 15:7; Ephesians 3:20; James 4:2-3; 1 John 3:22, 5:14-15.

Seek: 1 Chronicles 16:10; Psalms 14:2, 34:4, 40:16, 42:2, 53:2, 119:10, 45, 94; Proverbs 28:5; Daniel 9:3; Lamentations 3:25; Matthew 13:45; Hebrews 11:6

Knock: Luke 11:9-10, 12:36; Revelations 3:20

More Study

Job 36:22   John 14:17; 16:13   2 Corinthians 1:21, 22   1 John 2:20

I will daily put on the armor of God. 2 Cor. 10:3-6; Eph. 6:10-18

Note: This lesson will be covered in part 2, lesson 5 of this study.

I will set no unclean thing before my eyes, and I will flee from lust and sexual immorality. Job 31:1, 4; Ps. 119:11; Prov. 6:23-29; Matt. 5:27-28; 1 Cor. 3:16, 7:1, 8, 26, 32; Eph. 5:8-17; Phil. 4:8

Have you ever been watching a program on television or been on the internet when all of a sudden, without warning, you were abruptly faced with a scene, a commercial, or a pop-up ad that was completely offensive? Recently, I was checking my Facebook page when a lewd image on the screen popped up out of nowhere. I scrambled to get away from the page as quickly as possible. What is most disturbing is that the images we are exposed to just don't go away. They are impressed on our mind. The computer phrase "Garbage in, garbage out (GIGO)" reminds us that if we expose ourselves to garbage, that is what our mind will feed on. Here is another thought for "GIGO" introduced to me by a dear friend. GIGO also means "God in, God out." Expose yourself more to God; it will impact what comes out of your life.

DISCUSSION

Job 31:1-4 (NKJV) says:

> *I have made a covenant with my eyes; Why then should I look upon a young woman? ²For what is the allotment of God from above, And the inheritance of the Almighty from on high? ³Is it not destruction for the wicked, And disaster for the workers of iniquity? ⁴Does He not see my ways, And count all my steps?*

Questions: What are some examples of unclean or impure things that might come before your eyes? Why should it matter to you? What is the big deal with sexual immorality? How should you guard your eyes? Don't fall for the excuse, "We are all men. I was designed to appreciate God's beauty in women, so I can look as long as I don't touch!" Does that approach work very well?

Study Notes

_____

_____

_____

_____

_____

_____

_____

_____

_____

_____

Point: In Job 31:1-4, we see the huge impact our eyes have on our lives, whether we guard them or not. Realize that the eyes are a major sensory stimulus for men. Men's God-given natural attraction to women, coupled with visual imagery, can be and often is perverted, so Job protected his eyes. If you yield to temptation, destruction follows.

DISCUSSION

Proverbs 6:23-29 (NKJV) says:

> *For the commandment is a lamp, And the law a light; Reproofs of instruction are the way of life, [24]To keep you from the evil woman, From the flattering tongue of a seductress. [25]Do not lust after her beauty in your heart, Nor let her allure you with her eyelids. [26]For by means of a harlot A man is reduced to a crust of bread; And* **an adulteress** *will prey upon his precious life. [27]Can a man take fire to his bosom, And his clothes not be burned? [28]Can one walk on hot coals, And his feet not be seared? [29]So is he who goes in to his neighbor's wife; Whoever touches her shall not be innocent.*

Questions: Do you see how the eye was the first step to eventual devastation? What was the man warned of that would happen to him if he yielded?

Study Notes

_____

_____

_____

_____

_____

_____

_____

_____

_____

_____

_____

DISCUSSION

Ephesians 5:8-17 (NASB77) says:

> *for you were formerly darkness, but now you are light in the Lord; walk as children of light [9](for the fruit of the light consists in all goodness and righteousness and truth), [10]trying to learn what is pleasing to the Lord. [11]And do not participate in the unfruitful deeds of darkness, but instead even expose them; [12]for it is disgraceful even to speak of the things which are done by them in secret. [13]But all things become visible when they are exposed by the light, for everything that becomes visible is light. [14]For this reason it says, "Awake, sleeper, And arise from the dead, And Christ will shine on you." [15]Therefore be careful how you walk, not as unwise men, but as wise, [16]making the most of your time, because the days are evil. [17]So then do not be foolish, but understand what the will of the Lord is.*

Questions: Should our lives be different from the culture around us? If so, how? Do you know what pleases the Lord? Remember never to lose sight of what you have separated yourself from. Do you really want to go back to it?

Study Notes

_____

_____

_____

_____

_____

Application: Always be careful to ask yourself the following question: is what I am doing the best use of my time? The eye is the window to the soul and the portal to your imagination. Images can potentially grip your soul and spirit; they can shape your thought life. Your eyes are an unfiltered portal, providing images for your mind to feed on. Your conscience is the filter for your eyes, aided by your responsiveness to the promptings from the Holy Spirit not to look at something.

Sow good actions and then reap good results; sow bad actions and then reap bad results. Why should we willingly sow calamity, destruction, misfortune, or ruin into our life? Sin is so deceptive, and the true danger is hidden. Why should you live and conduct yourself like an evil, immoral person? None of us escape the watchful eye of God. Therein lies the challenge—your obedience. God desires obedience more than sacrifice; He desires you to willingly yield to the will of God for your life. Where your life ends up starts with your first choice to either move toward or away from that which is right. You can be purged of impurity, but the purging must come with sincere, heartfelt repentance in order to replace the impurity by a cleansing from the blood of Jesus over that sin. Do not just turn away from uncleanness; run from it as fast as you can run. Risk being different and out of "the know" concerning the rest of the culture around you. Substitute your lack of knowledge of the culture for the favor, grace, and mercy of God on your life. You choose!

Further Study

Genesis 34:2	2 Samuel 11:2	Psalm 24:3-4	Proverbs 22:11
Matthew 5:8	1 Corinthians 6:13	Philippians 2:15	1 Thessalonians 5:5
1 Timothy 1:5	2 Timothy 2:22	Titus 1:15	James 4:8
	2 Peter 2:14; 3:14	1 John 2:16.	

Additional Comments

"For we naturally love to do evil things that are just the opposite from the things that the Holy Spirit tells us to do; and the good things we want to do when the Spirit has his way with us are just the opposite of our natural desires. These two forces within us are constantly fighting each other to win control over us, and our wishes are never free from their pressures" (**Galatians 5:17** TLB).

What we are now discussing is no small matter! Your eyes are gateways into your mind. They directly affect your thoughts and inner man. Emotions are connected to images captured by the eyes and stored in the mind. Those connections produce a hold or a stronghold in your life that is very difficult to remove. A stronghold could also be thought of as territory that you stand on or control. It is yours to control, and no one else has a right to it unless it is surrendered or unless permission is given to another for full or partial control.

This ground is physical, emotional, and spiritual. In this struggle, we must recognize that when we sin, we give ground to the enemy. We give Satan permission to occupy parts of our lives. He then controls that territory. We are instructed not to give the devil an opportunity for control (Eph. 4:27). Romans 13:14 says, *"Make no provision for the flesh."* By giving ground to the enemy, we permit him to exercise influence over us by the sins and wrong behavior patterns we allow in our lives. Satan has no authority in a Christian's life, except that which is surrendered to him.

Each person has the ability to maintain control over his eyes and everything to do with this area of life. There are many opportunities to be influenced by evil spiritual entities that constantly bombard the mind through visual images. These evil entities are always seeking to establish a foothold for greater control of your thought life and actions. When we give ground to Satan, he will build a stronghold of false reasoning on that ground. According to 2 Corinthians 10:5, speculations, arguments, and every lofty thing comes against the knowledge of God. As long as Satan controls that ground, the individual will continue to make wrong choices. We give ground when we refuse to let go of our sin, to confess it, and to repent or turn away from it. When we surrender or give ground, the following things happen:

1) We get wrong ideas—strongholds

2) Which lead to wrong actions—sin

3) Which bring wrong results—tormentors (Matt. 18:34)

When Satan gets a firm enough foothold in a person's life he:

a) Turns **an act** of sin into

b) A **regular practice** of sin that

c) Degenerates into **a habit** which

d) Leads to **bondage.**

Job made a covenant with his eyes. Imagine how he recognized the dangers of allowing indiscriminate input to enter his mind. He worked to keep his thoughts pure, and his life was characterized by walking in a manner that pleased God. You can walk the same way Job walked if you are committed to the same diligence.

When you asked Jesus to be Lord of your life, you surrendered, yielded, and gave Him permission to take up residency on the territory or ground of your life. This didn't make Satan, the enemy of your soul and spirit, very happy. Satan's influence is often called the spirit of the world. You left that spirit behind to yield yourself to the Spirit of the Lord, the Holy Spirit. So ask yourself, "If I left this spirit of the world, can I or should I willingly set myself in front of it?"

A person must be united with the world to enjoy its pleasures. To enjoy worldly pleasures, the

Holy Spirit within you would have to yield Himself to the spirit of the world and create a bonding of spirits, which the Holy Spirit can never do. Double-mindedness is the result. A believer should be single-minded and committed to just one spirit, the Holy Spirit. We must not be half-hearted. We cannot be lukewarm in the fray of the battle. James 1:8 says of a half-hearted man, *"He is a double-minded man, unstable in all his ways."* If one is unstable, he is off balance and an easy pushover. We must be alert. I Thessalonians 5:8 says to be sober (alert) to the schemes of Satan.

The spirit of the world is constantly tempting you through every visual media outlet possible to yield the ground to Satan that you had already given to Jesus. Know this: you don't have to return to the old, dirty condition you left. Don't place yourself in a position to be tempted by the enemy. He is much too crafty and deceptive. He is skilled at patiently laying traps for unsuspecting believers. Yielding just one inch to the Enemy opens the door for his relentless assault to reclaim a place of influence in your life.

If a believer gives ground to the Enemy, the believer, in the power of the Holy Spirit, can reclaim the ground he has yielded. Taking back surrendered ground requires warfare and knowledge on how and what to do to reclaim the ground. Spiritual battles can only be won through the power of Jesus Christ (I Corinthians 2:14; Colossians 2:15).

Steps to Taking Back Surrendered Ground

a)   Ask God to reveal to you the first time you violated His moral law and began to give Satan ground in your life.

b)   Confess each sin God brings to your mind—I John 1:9

c)   Claim the blood of Jesus for cleansing—I Peter 1:18-19; Revelation 12:11

d)   Ask God to restore the surrendered ground—Psalm 23:3; 2 Corinthians 4:16

e)   Tear down strongholds with God's truth—2 Corinthians 10:4-5

f)   Transform your mind with the truth of God's Word—Romans 12:2; I Corinthians 2:16; Proverbs 23:7

g)   Fully forgive others—especially those who have offended you—Matthew 6:12, 14, 15

- A lack of forgiveness is surrendered ground to the enemy and becomes a stronghold used by Satan.

Biblical Steps to Freedom in Jesus Christ

1.   Remember Satan is a defeated foe.

2.   The cross of Christ renders him powerless.

3. The enemy has no power over God's people except that which we permit him to have.

4. The following are each parts to reclaiming your freedom in Christ.

    a) Genuine repentance of sin—2 Corinthians 7:10

    b) Take back surrendered ground

    c) Tear down strongholds—John 8.22; Revelation 12:9

    d) Build a tower of truth—Psalm 61:3; Proverbs 18:10; Psalm 18:1-3

    e) Take thoughts captive and be obedient to Jesus Christ—2 Corinthians 10:5

    f) Keep your conscience clear—I Timothy 1:5; Acts 24:16

    g) Daily put on your spiritual armor—Ephesians 6:10-18
        (Note: the armor of God will be fully studied in part 2, lesson 5)

        •   Until these steps becomes a daily pattern in your life, read Ephesians 6:10-18 first thing every morning.

Be diligent and ever attentive to the influences that are trying to establish a foothold in your life. Remember the story in Luke 11:24-26. This passage tells how evil spirits are cast out of a man and they try to return. Once you are freed from evil, unwanted influences, don't be naïve to think you will not be tempted by these influences again—often in a more aggressive manner. So, like the watchman or guard on the gate, do not fall asleep. You should be carefully watching for attacks. The consequences for a lack of alertness could be overwhelming.

Guard your eyes. Replace unwanted influences with positive, enriching images that are God-filled imagery. The enticement is relentless, so be relentless not to yield up ground to emotional attraction or appeal. Every time you pass through an assault from the enemy, your life's resolve becomes stronger, and your defensive wall more impenetrable. You are to be set apart, living a life that reflects who God is.

What is at stake here is who is in control of, who influences, or who affects your life. Make a covenant with your eyes!

Additional Reading

Matthew 12:22-29; 23:25	Luke 11:21-26	John 6:70; 13:2
Romans 12:2	1 Corinthians 3:17; 10:21	Galatians 5:16, 17
2 Timothy 1:9; 2:26	1 Peter 1:15; 3:8	2 Peter 2:20-22; 3:11
James 4:1-7	1 John 3:8-10	

Notes:

"The Lord is a warrior..."
Exodus 15:3 (NET)

Conclusion of Part 1

BEFORE WE CONTINUE OUR study and look at the symbolic parts and meanings of the Warrior Ring, let's reflect on the Warrior Covenant. There were sixteen "I wills" in the covenant. All were designed to get you to think about where you are currently in your life's walk before God and to challenge you to take action in the areas that you know need to be changed. The "I wills" remind you to love, honor, and seek God alone; you are to carry His love as you engage and live with your neighbor, not abusing your liberty but carrying it with discretion. You are to remember that you are not an island but accountable to your wife, if married, and to others. You are to be an example to your children and to others around you, because they are watching how you live. The decisions that you make become the ones they just might copy.

Acknowledge that you need God's wisdom, discernment, and understanding. Put off selfishness and live for others. There you will find your greatest fulfillment. Allow your character to develop patience, kindness, humility, forgiveness, and the other attributes of God's character. Discipline yourself to walk away from anything set before you that will cause you to stumble or compromise your integrity before others and God. Listen to the counsel and instruction from the Holy Spirit and remember that you are in a physical and spiritual battle against powers and demons that want to destroy you and the One you serve. Live daily by the Word of God because it reveals who God is. Know your God.

Develop a fear of God (Jeremiah 32:40); to fear Him is to revere Him. Fear does not mean that you cower before Him, but that you fully understand who God is, and that you realize there is none equal to Him. God is the starting place of all good things (Psalms 145:19; James 1:17). We must respect God because He judges good and evil (Ecclesiastes 12:13-14). We must be in awe of God because He holds the power of life and death (Psalms 145:20; Lamentations 3:22; Deuteronomy 32:39). We must revere God because doing so is for our own good (Jeremiah 32:39). Anything or anyone other than God Himself is an idol (Psalms 96:5). Worship and serve only Him.

Finally, remember:

*"The law of the Lord is **perfect**, converting the soul;*
*The testimony of the Lord is **sure**, making wise the simple;*
*The statutes of the Lord are **right, rejoicing the heart**;*

> *The commandment of the LORD is **pure, enlightening** the eyes;*
> *The **fear of the LORD is clean**, enduring forever;*
> *The judgments of the LORD are **true and righteous** altogether.*
> *More to be desired are they than gold;*
> *Yea, than much fine gold;*
> *Sweeter also than honey and the honeycomb.*
> *Moreover by them **Your servant is warned**,*
> ***And in keeping them there is great reward***" (Psalm 19:7-11 NKJV).

The bold font is added to emphasize the value and benefits of the Word of God and to show who God is and why He can be trusted and followed. He is perfect, sure, enlightening, encouraging, clean, true, righteous, and valued above all things. The way you set your priorities results in potentially great reward and fulfillment for your life.

Let's continue in our journey to follow God and become men after God's own heart!

The Warrior Covenant

"The Lord is a warrior…" (Exodus 15:3, NET)

I will, love the Lord with all my understanding, heart, soul, mind, and my strength and have no other gods before the Lord my God. Deut. 6:5; Ex. 20:3; Mark 12:30

I will, seek the Lord, His kingdom, and His righteousness first and foremost and then worship nothing other than the Lord God. Ex. 20:4; Deut. 4:35 (ESV); Is. 44:6 (ESV); Matt. 6:33; Rom. 1:25, 3:10-12, 21-24, 5:12-21, 12:1-2; 2 Cor. 5:21; James 1:14, 4.4, 1 John 2.15-17

I will, follow, honor, and submit to the plans and purposes designed by God for my life. Gen 1:28; Ps 139:1-18, 23-24; Eccl. 12:13; Is. 43:7; Jer. 29:11-13; Micah 6:8; John 4:23, 15:16; 1 Cor. 6:19-20; Eph. 1:4-12, 2:9-10; Phil. 3:9-10

I will honor my mother and father and all authority placed over my life. Ex. 20:12; Deut. 27:16a; Lev. 19:3a; Matt. 15:4; Rom. 13:1-7; Eph. 6:1-3; 1 Tim. 2:1-2; Titus 3:1; 1 Pet. 2:13-17

I will love, honor, and cherish my marriage and my wife. Deut. 5:18; Prov. 12:4a, 18:22; Eph. 5:25-33; Col. 3:19; Heb. 13:4; 1 Pet. 3:7

I will, if I have children, intentionally teach and, by God's grace and power, model for them the Word of God. Deut. 6:6-7, 11:18-31; Prov. 22:6; Col. 3:21

I will love and treat my neighbor the way I would like to be treated. Mark 12:31; Luke 6:27-42; Rom. 13:8-10; Gal. 5:13-15; James 2:8-9; 1 John 4:7-21

I will not allow my liberty or freedom in Christ to be a stumbling block to others, neither judging them nor causing others to fall away, lose faith, or blaspheme God because of my liberty. Rom. 14:12-23; 1 Cor. 8:4-13, 10:23-30; Gal. 5:13-14

I will be accountable to other men, to my wife, and to my family. Prov. 13:20, 17:17, 18:1, 27:17; Gal. 5:15-21, 6:1-5; 1 Thess. 5:11-15; Heb. 10:24; James 5:16

I will seek knowledge, wisdom, discernment, and understanding. 1 Kings 3:9, 12; Prov. 2:1-8, 3:13, 4:20-22, 19:20; Matt. 7:7-8; James 1:5-6

I will put off completely my selfish, sinful life, put on the new life found in Christ Jesus, and submit to the renewing of my mind, that He might sanctify me, having cleansed me by the washing of water with the Word. Eph. 4:22-24, 5:26; Col. 3:8-17; Rom. 12:1-2; James 1:21; 2 Cor. 5:17-19; Phil. 4:8-9

I will, by God's grace, commit to being patient and kind; not jealous, boastful, proud or rude; not demanding my own way; not irritable or keeping records of wrong; not taking part in injustice; not being self-willed, quick-tempered, or violent; not being greedy but hospitable, sober-minded, just, and self-controlled. 1 Cor. 13:4-7; Gal. 5:22-23; 1 Tim. 3:8-13; Titus 1:5-9

I will daily live by the Word of God through the power of the Holy Spirit. Ps. 19:7-14, 111:10, 119:2, 11, 97-98, 130, 105; Matt. 4:4; 2 Tim. 3:16-17; Heb. 4:12-13

I will listen to and seek counsel from the Holy Spirit. 1 Chr. 28:9; Prov. 8:1-19; Luke 2:25-27a, 4:1, 11:9-13; Rom. 8:26-27; 1 John 2:27, 5:14

I will daily put on the armor of God. 2 Cor. 10:3-6; Eph. 6:10-18

I will set no unclean thing before my eyes, and I will flee from lust and sexual immorality. Job 31:1, 4; Ps. 119:11; Prov. 6:23-29; Matt. 5:27-28; 1 Cor. 3:16, 7:1, 8, 26, 32; Eph. 5:8-17; Phil. 4:8

I, _____, pledge before God this _____ day of _____, 20___, to make every effort to walk in His grace with integrity, allowing Him to make me into the man who reflects the image of Christ Jesus for the glory of God.

"The LORD is a warrior..."
Exodus 15:3 (NET)

Part 2: The Warrior Ring

Lesson 1
Why Jesus and the Cross

THE CROSS OF CHRIST

IN 1984, POLISH COMMUNIST LEADER, Prime Minister Jaruzelski, ordered crucifixes to be removed from classroom walls, just as they had already been banned in factories, hospitals, and other public places, because there were not to be any displays of religious icons. Many Catholic bishops attacked the ban. It stirred waves of anger and resentment all across Poland. Ultimately, the government relented but still insisted that the law remain on the books. They agreed not to press for removal of the crucifixes, particularly in the schoolrooms.

But one defiant and unsympathetic Communist school administrator in Garwolin decided that the law was the law. So one evening he had seven large crucifixes removed from lecture halls where they had hung since the school's founding in the 1920s. Days later, parents entered the school and hung more crosses. The administrator promptly had them taken down.

The next day four hundred of the school's six hundred students staged a sit-in. When heavily armed, specially trained riot police arrived, the students were forced into the streets. Then they marched, crucifixes held high, to a nearby church where they were joined by 2500 other students from nearby schools for a morning of prayer in support of the protest. Soldiers surrounded the church. But the pictures from inside of students holding crosses high above their heads flashed around the world. So did the words of one priest who delivered the message to the weeping congregation that morning. "There is no Poland without a cross."

My brothers, it all begins at the cross. Without the cross, none of us would have any hope or chance for change in our lives. The cross both fulfilled one promise and began another—a promise to you and me that because of Christ and through Christ, our sins are forgiven. And now you can start fresh and be a new man. Do you need a fresh start or need to push your life's reset button? The cross is your beginning. Oh, the blood of Jesus, it washes me white as snow—nothing but the cross of Jesus. Let the following hymns enrich this message in your heart.

Alas! and Did My Savior Bleed *by Isaac Watts (1674-1748)*

Alas! and did my Savior bleed,
and did my Sovereign die!
Would he devote that sacred head
for sinners such as I?

REFRAIN: At the cross, at the cross,
where I first saw the light,
and the burden of my heart rolled away;
it was there by faith I received my sight,
and now I am happy all the day!

2. Was it for crimes that I have done,
he groaned upon the tree?
Amazing pity! Grace unknown!
And love beyond degree!
(Refrain)

3. Well might the sun in darkness hide,
and shut its glories in,
when God, the mighty maker, died
for his own creature's sin.
(Refrain)

4. Thus might I hide my blushing face
while his dear cross appears;
dissolve my heart in thankfulness,
and melt mine eyes to tears.
(Refrain)

5. But drops of tears can ne'er repay
the debt of love I owe.
Here, Lord, I give myself away;
'tis all that I can do.
(Refrain)

When I Survey the Wondrous Cross *by Isaac Watts (1674-1748)*

1. When I survey the wondrous cross
on which the Prince of Glory died;
my richest gain I count but loss,
and pour contempt on all my pride.

2. Forbid it, Lord, that I should boast,
save in the death of Christ, my God!
All the vain things that charm me most,
I sacrifice them to his blood.

3. See, from his head, his hands, his feet,
sorrow and love flow mingled down.
Did e'er such love and sorrow meet,
or thorns compose so rich a crown.

4. Were the whole realm of nature mine,
that were a present far too small;
Love so amazing, so divine,
demands my soul, my life, my all.

The Old Rugged Cross *by George Bennard (1913)*

1. On a hill far away stood an old rugged cross,
The emblem of suff'ring and shame;
And I love that old cross where the Dearest and Best
For a world of lost sinners was slain.

REFRAIN: So I'll cherish the old rugged cross,
Till my trophies at last I lay down;
I will cling to the old rugged cross,
And exchange it some day for a crown.

2. O that old rugged cross, so despised by the world,
Has a wondrous attraction for me;
For the dear Lamb of God left His glory above
To bear it to dark Calvary.

3. In that old rugged cross, stained with blood so divine,

A wondrous beauty I see,

For 'twas on that old cross Jesus suffered and died,

To pardon and sanctify me.

4. To that old rugged cross I will ever be true,

Its shame and reproach gladly bear;

Then He'll call me some day to my home far away,

Where His glory forever I'll share.

Do you have any burdens in your life brought on by your choices to sin and walk without God? Have your passions gotten away from you? Does pride drive your life? Have evil influences crept into your life? How does freedom sound to you—a fresh start in life, cleansed and set free from the stigma brought on by wrong choices? You can daily live your life, praising (joyfully living) and thanking God for a new beginning. Today is the day that change comes your way and you make all things right! It all starts at the cross of Jesus Christ on Calvary. Choose this day Whom you will serve.

Read Galatians 6:14 (TLB)

As for me, God forbid that I should boast about anything except the cross of our Lord Jesus Christ. Because of that cross, my interest in all the attractive things of the world was killed long ago, and the world's interest in me is also long dead.

DISCUSSION

What if there had never been a cross? What would that look like for your life? Would there be any impact? If so, share what it would be. If Jesus had not volunteered to die on the cross in your place, where would you be today?

Read Hebrews 12:1-3 (MEV)

Therefore, since we are encompassed with such a great cloud of witnesses, let us also lay aside every weight and the sin that so easily entangles us, and let us run with endurance the race that is set before us. ²Let us look to Jesus, the author and finisher of our faith, who for the joy that was set before Him endured the cross, despising the shame, and is seated at the right hand of the throne of God. ³For consider Him who endured such hostility from sinners against Himself, lest you become weary and your hearts give up.

What does the cross of Jesus Christ represent in your life? How personal is the cross to you? Can you share why?

Study Notes

_____

_____

_____

_____

_____

Read Genesis 3:1-13 (NKJV)

Now the serpent was more cunning than any beast of the field which the LORD God had made. And he said to the woman, "Has God indeed said, 'You shall not eat of every tree of the garden'?" ²And the woman said to the serpent, "We may eat the fruit of the trees of the garden; ³but of the fruit of the tree which is in the midst of the garden, God has said, 'You shall not eat it, nor shall you touch it, lest you die.'"

⁴Then the serpent said to the woman, "You will not surely die. ⁵For God knows that in the day you eat of it your eyes will be opened, and you will be like God, knowing good and evil."

⁶So when the woman saw that the tree was good for food, that it was pleasant to the eyes, and a tree desirable to make one wise, she took of its fruit and ate. She also gave to her husband with her, and he ate.

⁷Then the eyes of both of them were opened, and they knew that they were naked; and they sewed fig leaves together and made themselves coverings. ⁸And they heard the sound of the LORD God walking in the garden in the cool of the day, and Adam and his wife hid themselves from the presence of the LORD God among the trees of the garden.

⁹Then the LORD God called to Adam and said to him, "Where are you?"

¹⁰So he said, "I heard Your voice in the garden, and I was afraid because I was naked; and I hid myself."

¹¹And He said, "Who told you that you were naked? Have you eaten from the tree of which I commanded you that you should not eat?"

¹²Then the man said, "The woman whom You gave to be with me, she gave me of the tree, and I ate."

¹³And the LORD God said to the woman, "What is this you have done?" The woman said, "The serpent deceived me, and I ate."

DISCUSSION

What does the original sin of rebellion (defiance or disobedience) against God's instructions for Adam and Eve have to do with us today? How did God patch up (cover) Adam and Eve's disobedience? Why do you think there had to be a sacrifice involving the shedding of blood?

Study Notes

_____

_____

_____

_____

_____

Point: The following passage is rich with life lessons. Struggling with temptation is no joke. Recognize temptation and avoid its deception.

OBSERVATION

Genesis 3:1-13

V. 1: The serpent was *crafty* (sneaky, sly, evasive, devious, not straightforward but calculating, scheming with cunning underhanded plans, clever, tricky, intelligent, knowledgeable, deceptive, and not to be trusted). He probed for a weak spot in her defense. He questioned her walk with God and before others.

Vv. 2, 3: The woman unknowingly revealed a weak spot, a vulnerable point, an open place for the serpent to attack her life. Her innocence was at stake. Many times our innocence is at stake as well. When we completely trust, we're content and peaceful, and we don't question the command (direction, authority, or rule) of God.

V. 4: Deception started with a lie. Subtly Satan questioned the credibility of God. Just like Eve, in our weakness we don't respond in strength and confidence. Satan's lies cast doubt on our conviction. They challenge our understanding of the truth.

V. 5: Another lie continued the deception. The lie was based on shaky, unsound, and unclear reasoning. How could the serpent have known anything about what God knows? When lying starts, it sets off a chain of lies. One lie is spoken to cover the last one, and on it goes until the liar stops when confronted with truth.

V. 6: The tempted gave in to the tempter. Adam and Eve looked past being disobedient and valued the sin more than obedience. The object of temptation was valued above obedience to God. A cycle of sin started with Eve tempting Adam. She convinced (persuaded, won over, and influenced) him. In the same way, our desires cause us to give in to the dissatisfaction in our current state or place in life. Temptation never reveals the full consequence of the choice we are making. Sin is pleasing to the eye; it can seem enjoyable, gratifying, and pleasant. The temptation appeals to our desire to be independent, so we accept the lie that says, "Surely God wants me to be happy."

V. 7: Sin was deceptive, but once committed, the full weight of the wrong pressed upon Adam's and Eve's consciousness, and they felt the emotion of the wrong. What God had been protecting them from became clear. What have your eyes been opened to? We often try to cover up our wrong (again leading down a wrong path), but God already knows when we have made a wrong choice. Experience is often a harsh teacher. The tempter laughs at your wrong, while God grieves. God rejoices at your good choice, while the tempter shrinks away in the background of insignificance.

V. 8: Adam and Eve knew God's voice, but instead of listening to His voice, they yielded to the voice of another. We also feel confident while in sin, but ashamed (embarrassed, humiliated, or guilty) when approached by God. It's like a child who has done wrong and hears his parent calling. He doesn't want to be found out. His conscience is driving him to hide and not take ownership of his decision, so he crawls under the bed, thinking that because his parents are out of sight, he must be safe from discovery. The voice of God is calling out to us, but are we listening for it? What voices do you listen to?

V. 9: God was used to openly and freely walking with Adam and Eve, but something was different. Where were they? Why weren't they out in the open like on other days? It was time for them to come clean. Sin changes our behavior. Why are you hiding?

V. 10: Suddenly Adam feared God. He had never feared before. Sin removed the innocence from the relationship. Sin leaves a person *naked* (uncovered, unprotected). Every time sin comes our way, it tries to draw us away from the protection of God, our godly family, and our friends. The wolf or lion tries to separate the innocent prey from the herd or flock. Now exposed, the prey becomes easier to kill and destroy. Understand, the Enemy wants to destroy and kill you. He wants to steal from your anointing and from the calling of God on your life. He wants to eliminate you as a threat to his plans.

Vv. 11-13: Adam forgot the bone of my bone, flesh of my flesh praise he had given Eve, his helper. He forgot about the two of them becoming one flesh, cleaving to one another, and being "in this together." He threw her under the bus! Eve then did the same thing: she threw the serpent under the bus. Why not? She had just watched Adam do it to her. Adam wasn't being a very good role model or leader of his household at the time! Sin immediately tempts us to shift the blame. We fail to man up to our own choices, accepting the consequences of our decisions. Once in motion, the sin cycle can spin out of control.

If you're sincere about your daily Christian walk, enticement doesn't come directly at you.

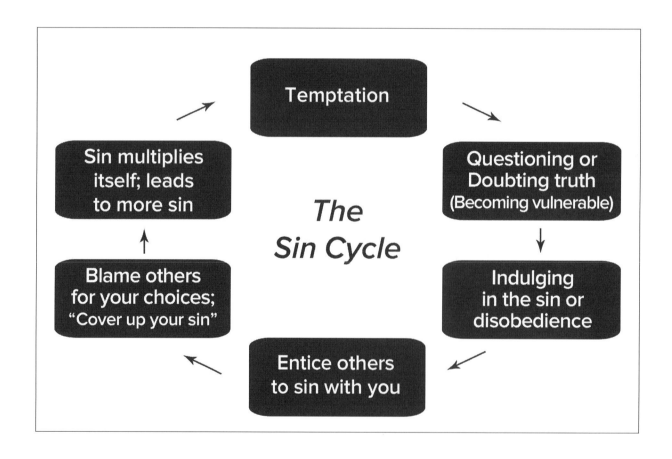

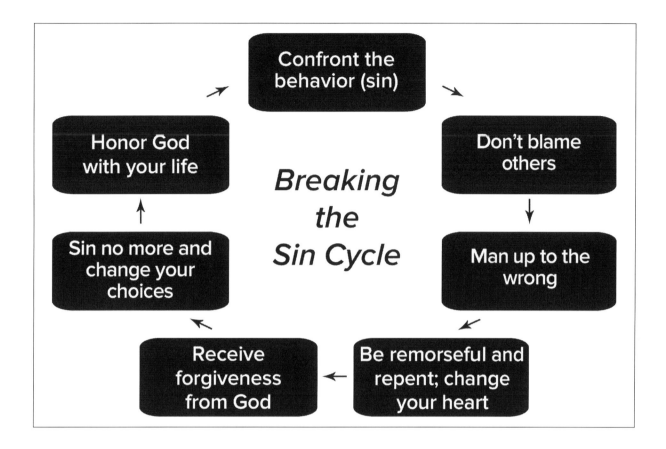

Read John 3:1-13 (NIV)

¹*Now there was a man of the Pharisees named Nicodemus, a member of the Jewish ruling council.*

²*He came to Jesus at night and said, "Rabbi, we know you are a teacher who has come from God. For no one could perform the miraculous signs you are doing if God were not with him."*

³*In reply Jesus declared, "I tell you the truth, no one can see the kingdom of God unless he is born again."*

⁴*"How can a man be born when he is old?" Nicodemus asked. "Surely he cannot enter a second time into his mother's womb to be born!"*

⁵*Jesus answered, "I tell you the truth, no one can enter the kingdom of God unless he is born of water and the Spirit.*

⁶*Flesh gives birth to flesh, but the Spirit gives birth to spirit.*

⁷*You should not be surprised at my saying, 'You must be born again.'*

⁸*The wind blows wherever it pleases. You hear its sound, but you cannot tell where it comes from or where it is going. So it is with everyone born of the Spirit."*

⁹*"How can this be?" Nicodemus asked.*

¹⁰"You are Israel's teacher," said Jesus, "and do you not understand these things?

¹¹I tell you the truth, we speak of what we know, and we testify to what we have seen, but still you people do not accept our testimony.

¹²I have spoken to you of earthly things and you do not believe; how then will you believe if I speak of heavenly things?

¹³No one has ever gone into heaven except the one who came from heaven—the Son of Man.

DISCUSSION

The cross is essential and indispensable to our daily walk of faith. Put yourself in Nicodemus' position for a moment. Just how unreasonable were his questions? What do you think about his questions? When did he come to Jesus? Would it have bothered you if someone had seen you with Jesus? What would be the questions you might be asking today?

Study Notes

_____

_____

_____

_____

_____

Read Numbers 21:7-9 (TLB)

⁷Then the people came to Moses and cried out, "We have sinned, for we have spoken against Jehovah and against you. Pray to him to take away the snakes." So Moses prayed for the people.

⁸Then the Lord told him, "Make a bronze replica of one of these snakes and attach it to the top of a pole; anyone who is bitten shall live if he simply looks at it!"

⁹So Moses made the replica, and whenever anyone who had been bitten looked at the bronze snake, he recovered!

Read John 3:14-21 (AMP)

¹⁴And just as Moses lifted up the serpent in the desert [on a pole], so must [so it is necessary that] the Son of Man be lifted up [on the cross],

¹⁵In order that everyone who believes in Him [who cleaves to Him, trusts Him, and relies on Him] may not perish, but have eternal life and [actually] live forever!

¹⁶For God so greatly loved and dearly prized the world that He [even] gave up His only begotten (unique) Son, so that whoever believes in (trusts in, clings to, relies on) Him shall not perish (come to destruction, be lost) but have eternal (everlasting) life.

¹⁷For God did not send the Son into the world in order to judge (to reject, to condemn, to pass sentence on) the world, but that the world might find salvation and be made safe and sound through Him.

¹⁸He who believes in Him [who clings to, trusts in, relies on Him] is not judged [he who trusts in Him never comes up for judgment; for him there is no rejection, no condemnation—he incurs no damnation]; but he who does not believe (cleave to, rely on, trust in Him) is judged already [he has already been convicted and has already received his sentence] because he has not believed in and trusted in the name of the only begotten Son of God. [He is condemned for refusing to let his trust rest in Christ's name.]

¹⁹The [basis of the] judgment (indictment, the test by which men are judged, the ground for the sentence) lies in this: the Light has come into the world, and people have loved the darkness rather than and more than the Light, for their works (deeds) were evil.

²⁰For every wrongdoer hates (loathes, detests) the Light, and will not come out into the Light but shrinks from it, lest his works (his deeds, his activities, his conduct) be exposed and reproved.

²¹But he who practices truth [who does what is right] comes out into the Light; so that his works may be plainly shown to be what they are—wrought with God [divinely prompted, done with God's help, in dependence upon Him].

DISCUSSION

Contrast **Numbers 21:7-9** (TLB) with **John 3:14-21** (AMP).

Point: The brown recluse spider or fiddleback spider is not much bigger than the size of a penny. Its bite is venomous. Often the bite is undetected or unnoticed. The signs of the bite show up slowly. First there is a rash and a small blister, but it is sometimes mistaken as harmless and not immediately treated. Then it starts to turn into a bigger problem. The skin changes color because toxins in the venom start to eat away the skin, and the skin dies. New skin does not grow back. The only hope is that the dying flesh, once treated, stops the decay process. Then a scar replaces the spot where there was once flesh.

Sin is much like the venom of the recluse spider. It slowly rots away the inside of a person. At first, you don't realize the consequences of sin. Often the sin is looked at as harmless, but left unchecked, sin can spiral out of control. The places that are touched by sin in a person's life are never the same.

Sin takes away years of life that are lost to time and never to be reclaimed. But there is a cure, and there is hope.

When you look to Jesus and lift Him up, the sting from the venom of sin in your life is drained out. You still may have the scar from the sin, but the consequence of sin is redeemed by the sacrifice of Jesus on the cross. Jesus died on the cross for all mankind. His blood redeems the scars of sinful, disobedient choices in your life. When you choose to lift up Jesus in your life and make Him Lord and Savior, change, hope, and recovery come to you for a brighter future and life.

Study Notes

_____

_____

_____

_____

_____

Read Matthew 10:37-39 (AMP)

37 He who loves [and takes more pleasure in] father or mother more than [in] Me is not worthy of Me; and he who loves [and takes more pleasure in] son or daughter more than [in] Me is not worthy of Me;

38 And he who does not take up his cross and follow Me [cleave steadfastly to Me, conforming wholly to My example in living and, if need be, in dying also] is not worthy of Me.

39 Whoever finds his [lower] life will lose it [the higher life], and whoever loses his [lower] life on My account will find it [the higher life].

Read 1 Corinthians 1:17, 18 (MEV)

17 For Christ did not send me to baptize, but to preach the gospel, not with eloquent words, lest the cross of Christ should be made of no effect.

Christ the Power and Wisdom of God

18 For to those who are perishing, the preaching of the cross is foolishness, but to us who are being saved it is the power of God.

DISCUSSION

What does taking up the cross mean to you? Are you willing to lay down your life (deny self) because of the cross? Do you expect any suffering from taking up the cross? If so, what type of suffering? Does Matthew 10:37 seem harsh to you?

Study Notes

_____

_____

_____

_____

_____

Read Philippians 3:7-9 (TLB)

⁷*But all these things that I once thought very worthwhile—now I've thrown them all away so that I can put my trust and hope in Christ alone.*

⁸*Yes, everything else is worthless when compared with the priceless gain of knowing Christ Jesus my Lord. I have put aside all else, counting it worth less than nothing, in order that I can have Christ,*

⁹*and become one with him, no longer counting on being saved by being good enough or by obeying God's laws, but by trusting Christ to save me; for God's way of making us right with himself depends on faith—counting on Christ alone.*

Read Galatians 2:19-21 (TLB)

¹⁹*for it was through reading the Scripture that I came to realize that I could never find God's favor by trying—and failing—to obey the laws. I came to realize that acceptance with God comes by believing in Christ.*

²⁰*I have been crucified with Christ: and I myself no longer live, but Christ lives in me. And the real life I now have within this body is a result of my trusting in the Son of God, who loved me and gave himself for me.*

²¹*I am not one of those who treats Christ's death as meaningless. For if we could be saved by keeping Jewish laws, then there was no need for Christ to die.*

DISCUSSION

What does being crucified with Christ mean to you? Why is it important that your righteousness (right standing) before God does not come through the law? What does the law represent in your life? Do you count all things as loss? Is there value in knowing Jesus and exalting the cross above everything? (This is a tough question, but one with eternal impact!)

Study Notes

_____

_____

_____

_____

_____

Application: What are you compelled to boast about? It might be your children, job, education, accomplishments, business, intellect, physical abilities, financial savvy, good deeds, community or church status. Whatever it is, how does it compare to what Jesus did for you by sacrificing His life and dying for you on the cross? The apostle Paul, in Galatians 2:20, counted his life no longer important when he completely surrendered to the lordship of Jesus Christ. He completely lived for serving Jesus. Jesus said that He was the way, the truth, and the life and that no man comes to the Father except through Him. He also said that the road is narrow that leads to real life transformation.

All of our **hope** begins at the **cross**. Jesus' sacrifice made change possible for all of mankind. The price that was paid—His sacrifice—was not small. Would you give your life voluntarily for another? This might be a tough question for you to answer, but through the substitution of Jesus on the cross, those who trust in Him, confess their sin, and turn from their broken relationship with God will be given a second chance. That chance is a new beginning in life, made possible because of the cross. This change can come at any time in an individual's life. Understand that you have to ask Jesus to give you this new life, found only in the cross, sacrifice, and blood of Jesus. Start fresh and begin your new life today!

Have you made Jesus Lord of your life? If you have, pursue Him with a passion to develop a daily, intimate relationship with Him. If you have not already accepted and surrendered to Jesus as Lord and Savior of your life and you would like to, then pray this prayer with me:

Lord Jesus, I thank You that You made it possible for my life to be different. Thank You that You took all of my wrong choices, my sinfulness, upon Yourself on the cross. Thank You that Your shed blood provided forgiveness for my sin. I now desire to yield myself and all of my plans, dreams, and life choices to You. Help me daily to live my life, and I ask You, Holy Spirit, to help me understand the Bible and apply it to all of my daily choices.

If you prayed this prayer, then reach out to other Christians so that they can come alongside of you to encourage you and walk with you. Then press on as you continue the rest of the study.

Further Study

Isaiah 53	Matthew 16:24, 26:28	Luke 9:23
John 5:24; 6:53; 8:28;12:25, 26	Acts 20:28	Romans 3:24, 25; 5:6-21; 6:23
1 Corinthians 1:29-31, 3:21	I Corinthians 10:16, 15:3, 45	2 Corinthians 5:18-21
Galatians 1:3-5; 3:13; 5:24; 6:14	Ephesians 1:7; 2:1-9, 13-19	Philippians 2:8; 3:8
Colossians 1:14, 20; 2:14	Titus 2:14	Hebrews 9:12, 14, 18, 22
Hebrews 10:5, 22; 12:1-3	Hebrews 13:20, 21	I Peter 1:18-21
1 John 1:7; 3:5, 8; 5:6	2 John 1:7	Revelation 1:5

Additional Comments

The cross and the blood of Christ are inseparable. I know that we have focused on the cross in this lesson, but let me simply remind you that without the shedding of blood on Christ's part, there would be no forgiveness of sin. There had to be a substitution—blood for blood. Our sinfulness had to be covered by the blood of the righteous substitute—Jesus. There is power in the precious blood of Jesus, the pure and spotless Lamb of God. Jesus' obedience to go to the cross, followed by the shedding of His blood, allowed those that believe in Him to confess their sins before Him and receive a fresh start in life. Read through and allow the following hymn to speak to you and reinforce this message.

Power in the Blood *by Lewis E. Jones (1899)*

Would you be free from the burden of sin?
There's power in the blood, power in the blood;
Would you o'er evil a victory win?
There's wonderful power in the blood.

CHORUS
There is power, power, wonder-working power
In the blood of the Lamb.
There is power, power, wonder-working power
In the precious blood of the Lamb.

Would you be free from your passion and pride?
There's power in the blood, power in the blood;
Come for a cleansing to Calvary's tide;
There's wonderful power in the blood.
[CHORUS]

Would you be whiter, much whiter than snow?
There's power in the blood, power in the blood;
Sin stains are lost in its life-giving flow;
There's wonderful power in the blood.
[CHORUS]

Would you do service for Jesus your King?
There's power in the blood, power in the blood;
Would you live daily His praises to sing?
There's wonderful power in the blood.
[CHORUS]

Notes:

_____

_____

_____

_____

_____

_____

_____

_____

"The Lᴏʀᴅ is a warrior..."
Exodus 15:3 (NET)

Part 2: The Warrior Ring

Lesson 2
Death to Self Through the Tomb,
Resurrection, and Baptism

ARETIRED MISSIONARY WHO HAD served faithfully in Africa for many years came upon a small baptismal service where a fellow missionary had taken three new converts to the center of a shallow stream and dug a hole in the sandy bottom so there would be enough water for the baptism. Even then, the new believers had to sit in the hole so there would be enough water to cover them for the baptism. The retired missionary saw what she'd expected. A few friends and family members had gathered to watch as the missionary in the river raised his hand, repeating familiar Scriptures before baptizing the converts. When the first convert came up out of the water, he began an excited and joyful time of shouting. The second convert did the same. The final convert also came up from the shallow water shouting for joy.

Afterward, the missionary who was watching the process asked about the unusual tradition. "Why all the shouting?"

"I haven't been able to completely communicate in this tribe's language," said the younger missionary. "They heard the Scripture I gave them, but they didn't understand the symbolic nature of it. When I told them that they would be 'buried with him by baptism into death…and we should walk in newness of life' (Romans 6:4), they actually thought baptism would kill them!"

"Let me ask you a question," the older missionary said. "If you thought baptism would kill you, would you be willing to get in the river?"

———

Now let me ask you the same question, "Would you be willing to follow Jesus into baptism if it meant you might be killed?" It cost Jesus His life to offer a new life to each of us. Are you willing to lay your life down for Him? The song goes something like this, "I surrender all, I surrender all, all to Jesus I surrender, I surrender all." Without holding back or without any reservation, would you continue on this journey of walking with Jesus?

Each of us lives in a culture that tries to influence our daily lifestyle. When Jesus was born and lived as a man, He introduced a new culture and lifestyle. He brought the culture of heaven to earth, and His daily lifestyle showed that it was possible to live differently here on earth. That fulfillment came through His death and resurrection. Where death is concerned, there are many ideas to be considered. The death that Jesus underwent was a very real and physical event; it was also a spiritual event. He defeated the grip of Satan's claim on mankind that had been caused by rebellion towards God. But why should that matter to you? So what? What did it all represent? Why was it so significant? Jesus' death brought an end to our inability to make a way for ourselves to God. When He said on the cross "It is finished," that meant that you and I didn't have to strive or work towards a right relationship with God because now it was possible to have a relationship through Him. It's important to realize that Jesus was fully man on the cross of Calvary. He knew that He was God's Son, doing the Father's will by going to the cross. Then followed His death and resurrection. Jesus demonstrated power over death. One has to die first though before there is a resurrection. When you die, there is absolutely nothing of yourself left inside of you to interfere with what God wants to do in your life. You are no longer trying to help God. When you come to that place, there is a complete death to self, and God can start to do a work in your life. Jesus' death and resurrection allowed you to have victory over your current life circumstances and the culture around you; it gave hope for a new and changed future.

When you choose to be baptized, you are identifying with Jesus' death and resurrection. You die to your former lifestyle and culture in exchange for His. You are saying you want to be a part of heaven's culture. You are now saved from past poor choices and given a fresh start. You are putting off your old way of living and putting on God's way of living. Selfishness for selflessness. Pride for humility.

Read John 12:24-26 (NIV)

> *I tell you the truth, unless a kernel of wheat falls to the ground and dies, it remains only a single seed. But if it dies, it produces many seeds.*
> *[25] The man who loves his life will lose it, while the man who hates his life in this world will keep it for eternal life.*
> *[26] Whoever serves me must follow me; and where I am, my servant also will be. My Father will honor the one who serves me.*

DISCUSSION

What do you think the word die means in this passage? Why must you lose your life? Give an example of how you deal with disliking something intensely in your present life. Does the full impact of identifying with Christ shake you up or give you any concern? The word die used here literally means "to die off, or to be dead." Pause and think about this for a moment: are you willing to walk down this road with Jesus? Will you be identified with Him and demonstrate it through public baptism?

Study Notes

_____

_____

_____

_____

_____

Additional Points: Consider the following Scriptures as they speak of what it means to completely surrender yourself to Christ.

Read Luke 9:23-26 (NKJV)

Then He said to them all, "If anyone desires to come after Me, let him deny himself, and take up his cross daily, and follow Me.

24For whoever desires to save his life will lose it, but whoever loses his life for My sake will save it.

25For what profit is it to a man if he gains the whole world, and is himself destroyed or lost?

26For whoever is ashamed of Me and My words, of him the Son of Man will be ashamed when He comes in His own glory, and in His Father's, and of the holy angels.

Read Mark 8:34-37 (TLB)

Then he called his disciples and the crowds to come over and listen. "If any of you wants to be my follower," he told them, "you must put aside your own pleasures and shoulder your cross, and follow me closely.

35If you insist on saving your life, you will lose it. Only those who throw away their lives for my sake and for the sake of the Good News will ever know what it means to really live.

36"And how does a man benefit if he gains the whole world and loses his soul in the process?

37For is anything worth more than his soul?"

Read Philippians 3:7-15 (TLB)

But all these things that I once thought very worthwhile—now I've thrown them all away so that I can put my trust and hope in Christ alone.

⁸Yes, everything else is worthless when compared with the priceless gain of knowing Christ Jesus my Lord. I have put aside all else, counting it worth less than nothing, in order that I can have Christ,

⁹and become one with him, no longer counting on being saved by being good enough or by obeying God's laws, but by trusting Christ to save me; for God's way of making us right with himself depends on faith—counting on Christ alone.

¹⁰Now I have given up everything else—I have found it to be the only way to really know Christ and to experience the mighty power that brought him back to life again, and to find out what it means to suffer and to die with him.

¹¹So whatever it takes, I will be one who lives in the fresh newness of life of those who are alive from the dead.

¹²I don't mean to say I am perfect. I haven't learned all I should even yet, but I keep working toward that day when I will finally be all that Christ saved me for and wants me to be.

¹³No, dear brothers, I am still not all I should be, but I am bringing all my energies to bear on this one thing: Forgetting the past and looking forward to what lies ahead,

¹⁴I strain to reach the end of the race and receive the prize for which God is calling us up to heaven because of what Christ Jesus did for us.

¹⁵I hope all of you who are mature Christians will see eye-to-eye with me on these things, and if you disagree on some point, I believe that God will make it plain to you.

Jesus is asking us to leave everything behind in exchange for His future for our life. Very scary, but full of hope and promise. God has a design for your life. Is eternity worth everything to you? It's not an easy question—pretty intense—but your choice has a lasting impact for your everyday living now. All of Jesus' disciples were faced with the same question presented to you. Remember Peter's response: "Thou art the Christ, the Son of the living God." Peter didn't know what his fate would be when he followed Jesus, but he gave his whole life to the Savior. He died to himself; you too must do the same. One of the ways to identify with Jesus is through baptism.

Read Romans 6:1-6 (TLB)

Well then, shall we keep on sinning so that God can keep on showing us more and more kindness and forgiveness?

²Of course not! Should we keep on sinning when we don't have to?

³For sin's power over us was broken when we became Christians and were baptized to become a part of Jesus Christ; through his death the power of your sinful nature was shattered.

⁴Your old sin-loving nature was buried with him by baptism when he died; and when God the Father, with glorious power, brought him back to life again, you were given his wonderful new life to enjoy.

⁵For you have become a part of him, and so you died with him, so to speak, when he died; and now you share his new life and shall rise as he did.

⁶Your old evil desires were nailed to the cross with him; that part of you that loves to sin was crushed and fatally wounded, so that your sin-loving body is no longer under sin's control, no longer needs to be a slave to sin.

DISCUSSION

What does being baptized mean to you? Death and turning away from your former attachments brings separation. What must you be separated from? An association, habit, business associate, or lifestyle? To *identify* means "to consider two or more things as being entirely or essentially the same." Do you see yourself as identifying with Christ? When you are baptized, you are doing the exact same thing Christ did. You are identifying with being raised up from and leaving behind your former life for the new life given to you from the Father. So now you are challenged and encouraged to live the way Jesus lives.

Study Notes

_____

_____

_____

_____

_____

Read I Corinthians 15:1-8, 12-14, 17, 19-21, 42-46, 50 (NKJV)

Moreover, brethren, I declare to you the gospel which I preached to you, which also you received and in which you stand,

²by which also you are saved, if you hold fast that word which I preached to you--unless you believed in vain.

³For I delivered to you first of all that which I also received: that Christ died for our sins according to the Scriptures,

⁴and that He was buried, and that He rose again the third day according to the Scriptures,

⁵and that He was seen by Cephas, then by the twelve.

⁶After that He was seen by over five hundred brethren at once, of whom the greater part remain to the present, but some have fallen asleep.

⁷After that He was seen by James, then by all the apostles.

⁸Then last of all He was seen by me also, as by one born out of due time.

¹²Now if Christ is preached that He has been raised from the dead, how do some among you say that there is no resurrection of the dead?

¹³But if there is no resurrection of the dead, then Christ is not risen.

¹⁴And if Christ is not risen, then our preaching is empty and your faith is also empty.

¹⁷And if Christ is not risen, your faith is futile; you are still in your sins!

¹⁹If in this life only we have hope in Christ, we are of all men the most pitiable.

²⁰But now Christ is risen from the dead, and has become the firstfruits of those who have fallen asleep.

²¹For since by man came death, by Man also came the resurrection of the dead.

⁴²So also is the resurrection of the dead. The body is sown in corruption, it is raised in incorruption.

⁴³It is sown in dishonor, it is raised in glory. It is sown in weakness, it is raised in power.

⁴⁴It is sown a natural body, it is raised a spiritual body. There is a natural body, and there is a spiritual body.

⁴⁵And so it is written, "The first man Adam became a living being." The last Adam became a life-giving spirit.

⁴⁶However, the spiritual is not first, but the natural, and afterward the spiritual.

⁵⁰Now this I say, brethren, that flesh and blood cannot inherit the kingdom of God; nor does corruption inherit incorruption.

DISCUSSION

What if the resurrection had never happened? Would that change anything in your life? How would you re-live your life if you could start all over? Through Jesus Christ, you are a new person when you confess your wrongs and choose Him! Can you embrace the transformation that your life has undergone through Christ?

Study Notes

_____

_____

_____

_____

_____

Application: Understand what Jesus did for all of mankind. The empty tomb is very, very significant. Inside the tomb, a process takes place—the transformation of a life. When a person dies to self, he goes from death to life with Jesus Christ. The voluntary yielding of oneself to God opens the door to the life-changing experience of a new life. This new life that passed through death can now live vicariously through the sacrifice of Jesus Christ. The act of being baptized symbolizes the transformation of your old life to your new life dedicated to Jesus Christ. Only you can voluntarily present yourself to the One you desire to serve. No one makes your will do what it doesn't want to do; you make the choice to yield. When you yield to something or someone, you consent to all that is associated with yielding. Jesus is offering you a brand new heart, mind, and life. Reach out and accept His gift. Leave the previous life that brought only disappointment, unfulfilled days, and hopelessness.

When you are baptized, you are making public your identification with Christ and are proclaiming that you are now associated with the death and resurrection of Jesus Christ. The death of Christ was only part of God's plan. Three days later came the resurrection! Without the resurrection, our faith is powerless. The death of Christ on the cross covered and forgave your past sinful life. The resurrection of Christ empowers you to live victoriously every single day of your life. The life you have now chosen is surrendered to God's plan and purpose for your life. Be accountable for the new days you have. What will you fill your new life with? What will you fill your time, your mind, and your priorities with now that you have been given a new start? Reflect Christ in all that you choose.

While serving in the French army, now deceased French writer Henri Barbusse (1874-1935) overheard a conversation in a trench full of wounded men during the First World War. One of the men, who knew he only had minutes to live, said to one of the other men, "Listen, Dominic, you've led a very bad life. Everywhere you are wanted by the police. But there are no convictions against me. My name is clear, so, here, take my wallet; take my papers, my identity, my good name, and my life and quickly hand me your papers that I may carry all your crimes away with me in death." We too have a similar offer made to us by God. Jesus offers a new life to those who will identify with him. Baptism is a part of the change we live out before others as we walk daily with Jesus.

Additional Benefits of Baptism:

(1) Regeneration (renewal). John 3:3, 5

(2) Remission (absolved from the consequences or suspension of the penalty) of sins (missing the mark). Romans 3:25, 1 Corinthians 6:11, Hebrews 10:22

(3) New spiritual relationship with Jesus Christ. You are now a part of the life that Jesus lives. Galatians 3:26-27

Further Study

Genesis 7:1-8, 19	Exodus 14:1-31	Psalm 51:1-12, 17
Acts 2:28-41, 8:26-38,	Acts 9:17-18, 22:12-16	Romans 6:7-14, 15-23
Romans 7:4-6	1 Corinthians 10:1, 2	2 Corinthians 8:5
Galatians 3:13, 5:24	Ephesians 4:17-24 (LB)	Philippians 3:10
Colossians 2:9-14, 3:1-15 (LB)	1 Peter 3:18-21	Hebrews 8:13

Notes:

_____

_____

_____

_____

_____

_____

_____

_____

_____

_____

_____

_____

_____

_____

_____

_____

"The LORD is a warrior..."
Exodus 15:3 (NET)

Part 2: The Warrior Ring

Lesson 3
Empowerment of the Holy Spirit

THE TRIUNE NATURE OF God is manifested through God the Father, God the Son, and God the Holy Spirit: all one and the same God. Most people are comfortable with God the Father. They recognize his attributes as Creator of the universe and all that is. He is omnipotent, omnipresent, and omniscient. He is the One Who spoke to Abraham as he journeyed from his homeland of Ur. He spoke to Moses on Mount Horeb, while Moses pastured his father-in-law Jethro's flock beneath the mountain of God. Then God called Moses to lead the Hebrews out of Egypt and through the Sinai Desert. God the Father later spoke to and was with Joshua as he led the children of Israel after Moses. God had used Joseph, and afterward He used both prophets and kings. Through these manifestations, we obtain and understand a picture of the Father.

Through Jesus, we see the manifestation of God the Son. Jesus had a miraculous birth: born of a virgin, making him fully God and man. He is the Lamb of God, sacrificing himself for all of mankind and redeeming our broken relationship with God. He is the suffering servant, taking on our sorrows and pain so that He can identify with our sufferings and pain. He was bruised and beaten for us, allowing Him to say, "By my stripes you are healed." Jesus wept, showing at the tomb of Lazarus that He empathized with our feelings of loss and that He loved greatly. Jesus never turned the children away, showing us that we have to have a childlike faith to see the kingdom of God. Jesus walked and talked with the Father every day. He modeled how our lives could be if we would follow His example. Jesus comforts us and never leaves us without providing for our cares. He told His disciples that unless He returned to the Father, He could not send the Holy Spirit.

God the Holy Spirit is more of a mystery. We are just not as comfortable walking daily with the Holy Spirit. I would like to explore this relationship. When we talk about the Holy Spirit, we have to talk about what role(s) He plays in the Holy Trinity in His relationships with the Father and the

Son. Some are afraid of this mystery, but there is no need to be afraid. After this lesson, you will have a better understanding of the operation of the Holy Spirit in our lives as Christians.

When we see the sun, we don't think of photosynthesis, but all around us every day its power (energy) is moving. Photosynthesis by definition is "the process by which green plants and some other organisms use sunlight to synthesize nutrients from carbon dioxide and water. Photosynthesis in plants generally involves the green pigment chlorophyll and generates oxygen as a by-product." You cannot see photosynthesis, but you can enjoy the effects of it when you see trees, plants, or flowers. You enjoy the fruit of an apple, orange, or pear tree. Maybe you have viewed the splendor of a large cluster of juicy, plump grapes hanging from a grapevine.

Without the sun's energy shining down daily on our planet, there would be no earth as we know it. This planet would be cold, without heat and lifeless. With the sun is life and life abundantly. Sunshine affects our emotions and personalities. The more we are exposed to the sun, the less gloomy our feelings are and the brighter our outlook is. The Holy Spirit daily moves in and through our lives much like the sun. You may not be able to see Him moving, but you can observe the fruit produced in a person's life.

Read John 15:5 (AMP)

I am the Vine; you are the branches. Whoever lives in Me and I in him bears much (abundant) fruit. However, apart from Me [cut off from vital union with Me] you can do nothing.

The Holy Spirit is the power flowing through the branch that produces in us a fruitful life that reflects the life Jesus lived. (This lesson is not meant to be exhaustive. There will be additional reading and study materials suggested at the end of the lesson if you want to learn more about living as Jesus did.)

One additional point to consider is that the Holy Spirit is foundational in our life, so don't rush through this lesson. Instead, meditate on the Scriptures discussed, carefully consider the questions asked, and finally, be open to what the Holy Spirit wants to teach you and reveal about Himself to you.

Jesus was born, He lived 30 years before starting His public ministry (his public ministry lasted three years), He was crucified and laid in a tomb for three days, and then He was resurrected from the grave by the power of the Holy Spirit. He lived and moved among the disciples and others for 40 days before He ascended to his Father. Before He went back to heaven, He instructed the disciples to tarry in the upper room so that the 120 present would receive the coming Promise from the Father. After 10 days, the presence or anointing of the Holy Spirit came upon those gathered in the upper room.

The first baptism is when we die to ourselves and then are raised again to the promise and hope of a transformed life because of and through Jesus. Next comes the dynamic relationship with the Holy Spirit, known as the second baptism, in our spiritual lives? The difference is that this baptism is by the Spirit of God, not water.

I want to weave a picture, letting the Scriptures show how critical the empowerment (filling up) of the Holy Spirit is in our daily walk. Without the filling of the Holy Spirit in our lives, we are only partially equipped to be victorious in the daily battles we may face. We are only partially equipped to fulfill the Great Commission for Jesus Christ and to reflect Him before others in our daily lives.

All Scripture is beneficial, meant to help us to be ready and to understand, so that we may be prepared to face our challengers with clarity and confidence and be able to defend the many different ideas expressed as truth. So let's continue to walk this journey together and explore the majestic wonder of the Holy Spirit's involvement in our daily lives.

Author's Note: This lesson is probably one of the weightiest in the study and definitely the longest. There was just too much to cover in one discussion, so I made a conscious decision to present a careful presentation of the Holy Spirit rather than a brief one. There will be four parts to the lesson.

Part 1: The Introduction of the Holy Spirit

A. *The Foretelling of the Holy Spirit*

Read Ezekiel 36:27 (NKJV)

I will put My Spirit within you and cause you to walk in My statutes, and you will keep My judgments and do them.

Read Zechariah 12:10 (NKJV)

"And I will pour on the house of David and on the inhabitants of Jerusalem the Spirit of grace and supplication; then they will look on Me whom they pierced. Yes, they will mourn for Him as one mourns for his only son, and grieve for Him as one grieves for a firstborn.

Read Joel 2:28-29 (NASB77)

"And it will come about after this That I will pour out My Spirit on all mankind; And your sons and daughters will prophesy, Your old men will dream dreams, Your young men will see visions. [29]*"And even on the male and female servants I will pour out My Spirit in those days.*

In each of these passages, it is important to see the relationship between God and mankind. Do you see a purpose developing? What is it?

Study Notes

_____

_____

_____

_____

_____

B. Jesus Ushers in the New Era of the Holy Spirit

Read Luke 2:25-32 (NKJV)

And behold, there was a man in Jerusalem whose name was Simeon, and this man was just and devout, waiting for the Consolation of Israel, and the Holy Spirit was upon him.

26And it had been revealed to him by the Holy Spirit that he would not see death before he had seen the Lord's Christ.

27So he came by the Spirit into the temple. And when the parents brought in the Child Jesus, to do for Him according to the custom of the law,

28he took Him up in his arms and blessed God and said:

29"Lord, now You are letting Your servant depart in peace, According to Your word;

30For my eyes have seen Your salvation

31Which You have prepared before the face of all peoples,

32A light to bring revelation to the Gentiles, And the glory of Your people Israel."

DISCUSSION

What can you observe from Simeon's life? What is significant about what he says in this passage? How is the Holy Spirit operating in this passage?

Study Notes

_____

_____

_____

_____

_____

Read Matthew 3:11 (AMP)

I indeed baptize you in (with) water because of repentance [that is, because of your changing your minds for the better, heartily amending your ways, with abhorrence of your past sins]. But He Who is coming after me is mightier than I, Whose sandals I am not worthy or fit to take off or carry; He will baptize you with the Holy Spirit and with fire.

Read John 1:33 (NKJV)

I did not know Him, but He who sent me to baptize with water said to me, 'Upon whom you see the Spirit descending, and remaining on Him, this is He who baptizes with the Holy Spirit.'

DISCUSSION

What does John the Baptist say about Himself? What does he say about Jesus? The baptism of Jesus is the beginning of a new time. Jesus will baptize in the power of the Holy Spirit.

Study Notes

_____

_____

_____

_____

_____

C. Jesus Starts Talking about the Promise of the Holy Spirit

As we focus on the ministry of Jesus, we see that for three years He traveled with and taught both His disciples and the crowds that gathered around Him. He showed them what was possible when a man walked in the direction and purpose of God. Everything seemed perfect for the disciples; they had the Son of God instructing them every day. They watched Him operate in the power of God. They witnessed miracle after miracle. Even under these conditions, they seemed confused over who Jesus was and why He came and lived among them. Jesus knew these concerns and answered the questions of the disciples as they presented themselves.

The disciples saw Him walk on water, heal the sick, open the eyes of the blind, and raise the dead. Jesus knew that every event of His life was to fulfil a plan and purpose. The disciples didn't put it all together until later, after the resurrection and ascension.

Jesus was in such close communion with the Father that He knew there was a timeline. He knew that within that timeline, the disciples would have to be prepared to stand on their own. They would have to be empowered. Jesus started to transition by telling the disciples about how the Holy Spirit would operate in their lives.

Read John 14:6 (NKJV)

Jesus said to him, "I am the way, the truth, and the life. No one comes to the Father except through Me.

Note: Jesus established that He was the only way to the Father.

DISCUSSION

Why is this so important? What are some of the other lies competing to take Jesus' place as the only way to the Father? Can you share some of your experiences or exposures to these other lies and what that was like for you? How did you break free from those influences on your life?

Study Notes

_____

_____

_____

_____

_____

Read John 14:12-14 (NKJV)

"Most assuredly, I say to you, he who believes in Me, the works that I do he will do also; and greater works than these he will do, because I go to My Father.
13 And whatever you ask in My name, that I will do, that the Father may be glorified in the Son.
14 If you ask anything in My name, I will do it.

DISCUSSION

What works did Jesus do while on earth? How do you feel when the Bible says His followers will do the same works as Jesus did? Do you have a hard time processing that you can do greater works than Jesus? What is the purpose for your doing these greater works?

Read John 14:15-18 (NKJV)

"If you love Me, keep My commandments.

¹⁶And I will pray the Father, and He will give you another Helper, that He may abide with you forever—

¹⁷the Spirit of truth, whom the world cannot receive, because it neither sees Him nor knows Him; but you know Him, for He dwells with you and will be in you.

¹⁸I will not leave you orphans; I will come to you."

DISCUSSION

Do you really love Jesus with your complete, undivided heart? What commandments is Jesus asking us to keep in our lives? Can you keep them in your own strength? What do you think about or what description do you associate with a helper? Does it comfort you to know that the Holy Spirit (the Helper) will walk with you forever? Why can't the world receive the Holy Spirit?

Study Notes

_____

_____

_____

_____

_____

Read John 14:26, 27 (NKJV)

But the Helper, the Holy Spirit, whom the Father will send in My name, He will teach you all things, and bring to your remembrance all things that I said to you.

²⁷Peace I leave with you, My peace I give to you; not as the world gives do I give to you. Let not your heart be troubled, neither let it be afraid.

Read John 15:26 (AMP)

But when the Comforter (Counselor, Helper, Advocate, Intercessor, Strengthener, Standby) comes, Whom I will send to you from the Father, the Spirit of Truth Who comes (proceeds) from the Father, He [Himself] will testify regarding Me.

Read John 16:5-7 (NKJV)

"But now I go away to Him who sent Me, and none of you asks Me, 'Where are You going?'

⁶But because I have said these things to you, sorrow has filled your heart.

⁷Nevertheless I tell you the truth. It is to your advantage that I go away; for if I do not go away, the Helper will not come to you; but if I depart, I will send Him to you."

Read 1 John 2:27 (NKJV)

But the anointing which you have received from Him abides in you, and you do not need that anyone teach you; but as the same anointing teaches you concerning all things, and is true, and is not a lie, and just as it has taught you, you will abide in Him.

DISCUSSION

Why were the disciples troubled? Of what were they afraid? The presence of the Holy Spirit in our lives is referred to as the anointing. Can you describe in your words what the anointing is? What does the Holy Spirit do in and through our daily lives? To what advantage to the disciples was it for Jesus to go away? At the time, I'm not sure they saw it as an advantage. Don't you think they liked it the way it was before—having Jesus around every day and following His lead? They might have seen this change as being thrown into the deep end of a swimming pool when they did not know how to swim. How can the Holy Spirit today comfort our concerns?

Note: Observe the different roles the Holy Spirit takes on in these verses.

Study Notes

_____

_____

_____

_____

_____

D. Asking for and Waiting to Receive the Holy Spirit

The Holy Spirit does not impose Himself upon you. You have to invite Him into your life. You have to take the first step by asking and opening the door of your life to Him. You have to be relentless when asking for the Holy Spirit.

Read Luke 11:9-13 (AMP)

So I say to you, Ask and keep on asking and it shall be given you; seek and keep on seeking and you shall find; knock and keep on knocking and the door shall be opened to you.

¹⁰For everyone who asks and keeps on asking receives; and he who seeks and keeps on seeking finds; and to him who knocks and keeps on knocking, the door shall be opened.

¹¹What father among you, if his son asks for a loaf of bread, will give him a stone; or if he asks for a fish, will instead of a fish give him a serpent?

¹²Or if he asks for an egg, will give him a scorpion?

¹³If you then, evil as you are, know how to give good gifts [gifts that are to their advantage] to your children, how much more will your heavenly Father give the Holy Spirit to those who ask and continue to ask Him!

Read Philippians 4:6, 7 (NKJV)

Be anxious for nothing, but in everything by prayer and supplication, with thanksgiving, let your requests be made known to God;

⁷and the peace of God, which surpasses all understanding, will guard your hearts and minds through Christ Jesus.

Read 1 John 5:14, 15 (AMP)

And this is the confidence (the assurance, the privilege of boldness) which we have in Him: [we are sure] that if we ask anything (make any request) according to His will (in agreement with His own plan), He listens to and hears us.

¹⁵And if (since) we [positively] know that He listens to us in whatever we ask, we also know [with settled and absolute knowledge] that we have [granted us as our present possessions] the requests made of Him.

Note: Ask with confidence and persistence until you receive the full and complete power of the Holy Spirit in your life.

DISCUSSION

The Father wants to give you the baptism (in-filling) of the Holy Spirit. Have you received the baptism of the Holy Spirit in your life? If not, why not ask for the Holy Spirit to come into your life? If you have received the Holy Spirit, can you share your experience of receiving the Holy Spirit?

Study Notes

_____

_____

_____

_____

Read Acts 1:4, 5 (NKJV)

And being assembled together with them, He commanded them not to depart from Jerusalem, but to wait for the Promise of the Father, "which," He said, "you have heard from Me;

⁵for John truly baptized with water, but you shall be baptized with the Holy Spirit not many days from now."

Read Acts 1:8 (NKJV)

"But you shall receive power when the Holy Spirit has come upon you; and you shall be witnesses to Me in Jerusalem, and in all Judea and Samaria, and to the end of the earth."

Read Acts 2:1-4 (TLB)

Seven weeks had gone by since Jesus' death and resurrection, and the Day of Pentecost had now arrived. As the believers met together that day,

²suddenly there was a sound like the roaring of a mighty windstorm in the skies above them and it filled the house where they were meeting.

³Then, what looked like flames or tongues of fire appeared and settled on their heads.

⁴And everyone present was filled with the Holy Spirit and began speaking in languages they didn't know, for the Holy Spirit gave them this ability.

Note: Fifty days after the death and crucifixion of Jesus on the cross, the disciples and others, a total of 120, waited for the Holy Spirit to come and manifest Himself. The day of Jesus' death corresponded with the celebration of the Passover and the manifestation of the Holy Spirit with the Feast of Pentecost or First Fruits observed by the Hebrews in the Old Testament. We have the benefit of seeing all of Scripture laid out before us. Because there are approximately fifty days between Passover and the Feast of Pentecost, we can figure out that those gathered in the upper room were there for ten days. However, at the time the book of Acts was written, none of those assembled had any idea what or when the manifestation would be demonstrated before their lives. They were obedient to wait, as Jesus told them to, to receive the Promise from the Father. This one event set in motion the empowerment of the Holy Spirit in and through the lives of believers. Without the Holy Spirit resting on our lives, we would not have the ability to effectively carry out the Great Commission of Christ. Don't be afraid of what God might do through or manifest in your life. Press in and desire for more of the Holy Spirit in your life.

DISCUSSION

What do you imagine was going through the minds of those gathered together in the upper room? Don't you think their emotions were all over the place. One moment they were up, and the next they were down. Do you think those gathered there were anxious? How do you think they passed the time while they waited? None of them knew exactly how long they would have to wait. Do you think that time was needed to both prepare and cleanse the hearts and minds of those waiting to receive the Holy Spirit? Why? Imagine being in a room with 120 people. Then all of a sudden, without notice, you hear a sound like a freight train roaring all around you. Do you think you would be scared? What happened after the coming of the Holy Spirit? Why and for what purpose?

Study Notes

_____

_____

_____

_____

_____

Read Hebrews 11:1 (AMP)

> *NOW FAITH is the assurance (the confirmation, the title deed) of the things [we] hope for, being the proof of things [we] do not see and the conviction of their reality [faith perceiving as real fact what is not revealed to the senses].*

Note: It is this same faith that we exercise to receive Jesus as Lord of our lives. It is by this same faith too that we receive the presence, the filling, and the operation of the Holy Spirit in our lives.

ADDITIONAL THOUGHTS

Read Acts 2:1-13 (NASB77)
> *And when the day of Pentecost had come, they were all together in one place.*
> *²And suddenly there came from heaven a noise like a violent, rushing wind, and it filled the whole house where they were sitting.*
> *³And there appeared to them tongues as of fire distributing themselves, and they rested on each one of them.*
> *⁴And they were all filled with the Holy Spirit and began to speak with other tongues, as the Spirit was giving them utterance.*
> *⁵Now there were Jews living in Jerusalem, devout men, from every nation under heaven.*

⁶And when this sound occurred, the multitude came together, and were bewildered, because they were each one hearing them speak in his own language.

⁷And they were amazed and marveled, saying, " Why, are not all these who are speaking Galilcans?

⁸"And how is it that we each hear them in our own language to which we were born?

⁹"Parthians and Medes and Elamites, and residents of Mesopotamia, Judea and Cappadocia, Pontus and Asia,

¹⁰Phrygia and Pamphylia, Egypt and the districts of Libya around Cyrene, and visitors from Rome, both Jews and proselytes,

¹¹Cretans and Arabs—we hear them in our own tongues speaking of the mighty deeds of God."

¹²And they all continued in amazement and great perplexity, saying to one another, "What does this mean?"

¹³But others were mocking and saying, " They are full of sweet wine."

DISCUSSION

Why do you think that **all** and not just **some** of those gathered in the upper room were filled with the Holy Spirit? What implication does this have for believers today in our modern culture?

What do you think caused the confusion in the crowd? It's easy to dismiss a move from God. Why was there mocking? Have you ever been guilty of dismissing a move from God simply because you might not have understood it? Can you share a move of God you personally experienced, either embracing or dismissing it?

Study Notes

_____

_____

_____

_____

_____

Read Acts 2:38 (NASB77)

And Peter said to them, " Repent, and let each of you be baptized in the name of Jesus Christ for the forgiveness of your sins; and you shall receive the gift of the Holy Spirit.

Read Acts 19:1-7 (NASB77)

And it came about that while Apollos was at Corinth, Paul having passed through the upper country came to Ephesus, and found some disciples,

²and he said to them, " Did you receive the Holy Spirit when you believed?" And they said to him, "No, we have not even heard whether there is a Holy Spirit."

³And he said, "Into what then were you baptized?" And they said, " Into John's baptism."

⁴And Paul said, " John baptized with the baptism of repentance, telling the people to believe in Him who was coming after him, that is, in Jesus."

⁵And when they heard this, they were baptized in the name of the Lord Jesus.

⁶And when Paul had laid his hands upon them, the Holy Spirit came on them, and they began speaking with tongues and prophesying.

⁷And there were in all about twelve men.

DISCUSSION

What must you do first to receive the baptism of the Holy Spirit? Is it possible to live without the fullness of the Holy Spirit in one's life? How much of the Holy Spirit do you want in your life?

Study Notes

_____

_____

_____

_____

_____

Part 2: The Holy Spirit Bridges the Gap Between Jesus and Our Daily Walk

A. Embrace the Holy Spirit in Your Daily Life

Read John 4:21-24 (NKJV)

Jesus said to her, "Woman, believe Me, the hour is coming when you will neither on this mountain, nor in Jerusalem, worship the Father.

²²You worship what you do not know; we know what we worship, for salvation is of the Jews.

²³But the hour is coming, and now is, when the true worshipers will worship the Father in spirit and truth; for the Father is seeking such to worship Him.

²⁴God is Spirit, and those who worship Him must worship in spirit and truth."

Read John 6:63 (NKJV)

It is the Spirit who gives life; the flesh profits nothing. The words that I speak to you are spirit, and they are life.

DISCUSSION

How should we daily worship God? How does the Holy Spirit help us understand worship? Can you completely trust enough to lay aside your own desires?

Study Notes

_____

_____

_____

_____

_____

B. *Daily Becoming Dependent upon the Holy Spirit*

Read John 5:19 (AMP)

So Jesus answered them by saying, I assure you, most solemnly I tell you, the Son is able to do nothing of Himself (of His own accord); but He is able to do only what He sees the Father doing, for whatever the Father does is what the Son does in the same way [in His turn].

Read John 5:30 (AMP)

I am able to do nothing from Myself [independently, of My own accord—but only as I am taught by God and as I get His orders]. Even as I hear, I judge [I decide as I am bidden to decide. As the voice comes to Me, so I give a decision], and My judgment is right (just, righteous), because I do not seek or consult My own will [I have no desire to do what is pleasing to Myself, My own aim, My own purpose] but only the will and pleasure of the Father Who sent Me.

Read Romans 8:1-10 (NKJV)

There is therefore now no condemnation to those who are in Christ Jesus, who do not walk according to the flesh, but according to the Spirit.

²For the law of the Spirit of life in Christ Jesus has made me free from the law of sin and death.

³For what the law could not do in that it was weak through the flesh, God did by sending His own Son in the likeness of sinful flesh, on account of sin: He condemned sin in the flesh,

⁴that the righteous requirement of the law might be fulfilled in us who do not walk according to the flesh but according to the Spirit.

⁵For those who live according to the flesh set their minds on the things of the flesh, but those who live according to the Spirit, the things of the Spirit.

⁶For to be carnally minded is death, but to be spiritually minded is life and peace.

⁷Because the carnal mind is enmity against God; for it is not subject to the law of God, nor indeed can be.

⁸So then, those who are in the flesh cannot please God.

⁹But you are not in the flesh but in the Spirit, if indeed the Spirit of God dwells in you. Now if anyone does not have the Spirit of Christ, he is not His.

¹⁰And if Christ is in you, the body is dead because of sin, but the Spirit is life because of righteousness.

Read Romans 8:11 (NKJV)

But if the Spirit of Him who raised Jesus from the dead dwells in you, He who raised Christ from the dead will also give life to your mortal bodies through His Spirit who dwells in you.

Read John 15:26 (NKJV)

"But when the Helper comes, whom I shall send to you from the Father, the Spirit of truth who proceeds from the Father, He will testify of Me.

Read John 16:12-15 (AMP)

I have still many things to say to you, but you are not able to bear them or to take them upon you or to grasp them now.

¹³But when He, the Spirit of Truth (the Truth-giving Spirit) comes, He will guide you into all the Truth (the whole, full Truth). For He will not speak His own message [on His own authority]; but He will tell whatever He hears [from the Father; He will give the message that has been given to Him], and He will announce and declare to you the things that are to come [that will happen in the future].

¹⁴He will honor and glorify Me, because He will take of (receive, draw upon) what is Mine and will reveal (declare, disclose, transmit) it to you.

¹⁵Everything that the Father has is Mine. That is what I meant when I said that He [the Spirit] will take the things that are Mine and will reveal (declare, disclose, transmit) it to you.

Read Ephesians 2:18 (NKJV)

For through Him we both have access by one Spirit to the Father.

Read 1 John 2:25-27 (NASB77)

And this is the promise which He Himself made to us: eternal life.

²⁶These things I have written to you concerning those who are trying to deceive you.

²⁷And as for you, the anointing which you received from Him abides in you, and you have no need for anyone to teach you; but as His anointing teaches you about all things, and is true and is not a lie, and just as it has taught you, you abide in Him.

DISCUSSION

Reflecting on these verses, what ability do you have in your own strength? In your own words, describe the relationship model Jesus had with the Father. What was Jesus listening for? Do you think He had to wait for answers from the Father? Why? What was Jesus being taught? Whose will was Jesus fulfilling? Does this thought change your priorities? How? Can you share your thoughts? How do you think Jesus came to the place where He could say that He had no desire to please Himself? What does it mean to walk by the Spirit? Can you say you walk daily by the power of the Holy Spirit? How do you cultivate your relationship with the Holy Spirit? Describe the two types of minds mentioned: the carnal and the spiritual mind.

What does it mean to you that the same Spirit that raised Jesus from the dead also dwells or lives with you? Do you grasp that the resurrection power that raised Jesus from the dead abides in you? What do you think about that truth? Describe what it means to you that the Holy Spirit will be a guide. What is the Holy Spirit pointing our lives to daily? Who are we to honor? Everything that is the Father's is given to Jesus, and Jesus says that He is giving it to us. What does this everything include?

Study Notes

_____

_____

_____

_____

_____

C. Our Bodies Are the Temple of the Holy Spirit

Read Romans 8:12-17 (MEV)

Therefore, brothers, we are debtors not to the flesh, to live according to the flesh.

¹³For if you live according to the flesh, you will die, but if through the Spirit you put to death the deeds of the body, you will live.

¹⁴For as many as are led by the Spirit of God, these are the sons of God.

¹⁵For you have not received the spirit of slavery again to fear. But you have received the Spirit of adoption, by whom we cry, "Abba, Father."

¹⁶The Spirit Himself bears witness with our spirits that we are the children of God,

¹⁷and if children, then heirs: heirs of God and joint-heirs with Christ, if indeed we suffer with Him, that we may also be glorified with Him.

Read 1 Corinthians 3:16 (NASB77)

Do you not know that you are a temple of God, and that the Spirit of God dwells in you?

Read 1 Corinthians 6:17, 19-20 (NASB77)

But the one who joins himself to the Lord is one spirit with Him.

¹⁹Or do you not know that your body is a temple of the Holy Spirit who is in you, whom you have from God, and that you are not your own?

²⁰For you have been bought with a price: therefore glorify God in your body.

DISCUSSION

What are your thoughts about your body as the temple of the Holy Spirit? Is the meaning physical, spiritual, or both? How so? As a son of God, should you live any differently than you are currently living? Does being a son of God affect your thinking? In what ways has your thinking changed? Explain why? The Holy Spirit confirms our sonship. We no longer have to yield to our flesh nature (character). How does the Holy Spirit help us deny our urges to give in to ungodly choices? How do we crucify the flesh? Can you share an example of how that works for you? Why are we warned not to walk by or according to the flesh?

What does it mean to be adopted? What are your rights as an adopted son? *Abba* means "daddy." It's an endearing expression, indicating that our Heavenly Father affectionately cares for us. You are one with the entirety of God (the Father, Son, and Holy Spirit), joined together with Him. Should you keep company with Him any differently than you are right now?

Study Notes

_____

_____

_____

_____

Part 3: Listening to and Being Empowered by the Holy Spirit

A. How Should You Respond When the Holy Spirit Speaks?

Read Luke 12:11, 12 (NKJV)

"Now when they bring you to the synagogues and magistrates and authorities, do not worry about how or what you should answer, or what you should say.

¹²For the Holy Spirit will teach you in that very hour what you ought to say."

Read Acts 11:12 (NKJV)

Then the Spirit told me to go with them, doubting nothing. Moreover these six brethren accompanied me, and we entered the man's house.

Read Acts 13:1-3 (NKJV)

Now in the church that was at Antioch there were certain prophets and teachers: Barnabas, Simeon who was called Niger, Lucius of Cyrene, Manaen who had been brought up with Herod the tetrarch, and Saul.

²As they ministered to the Lord and fasted, the Holy Spirit said, "Now separate to Me Barnabas and Saul for the work to which I have called them."

³Then, having fasted and prayed, and laid hands on them, they sent them away.

Read Acts 16:6, 7 (NKJV)

Now when they had gone through Phrygia and the region of Galatia, they were forbidden by the Holy Spirit to preach the word in Asia.

⁷After they had come to Mysia, they tried to go into Bithynia, but the Spirit did not permit them.

DISCUSSION

Do you see the Holy Spirit moving in these passages? The Holy Spirit always seems to be on time. How do you see the Holy Spirit demonstrating His power in these passages? Often we don't know whom we will speak to on any given day. So how should we prepare for talking with others? What should our response be when the Holy Spirit speaks to us? Should we be willing to accept a no instead of a yes from the Holy Spirit at times? Why?

Study Notes

_____

_____

_____

_____

_____

B. *The Holy Spirit Helps Us as We Pray:*

Read Romans 8:25-29 (AMP)

But if we hope for what is still unseen by us, we wait for it with patience and composure.

²⁶So too the [Holy] Spirit comes to our aid and bears us up in our weakness; for we do not know what prayer to offer nor how to offer it worthily as we ought, but the Spirit Himself goes to meet our supplication and pleads in our behalf with unspeakable yearnings and groanings too deep for utterance.

²⁷And He Who searches the hearts of men knows what is in the mind of the [Holy] Spirit [what His intent is], because the Spirit intercedes and pleads [before God] in behalf of the saints according to and in harmony with God's will.

²⁸We are assured and know that [God being a partner in their labor] all things work together and are [fitting into a plan] for good to and for those who love God and are called according to [His] design and purpose.

²⁹For those whom He foreknew [of whom He was aware and loved beforehand], He also destined from the beginning [foreordaining them] to be molded into the image of His Son [and share inwardly His likeness], that He might become the firstborn among many brethren.

Read 1 Corinthians 2:9-16 (MEV)

But as it is written, "Eye has not seen, nor ear heard, nor has it entered into the heart of man the things which God has prepared for those who love Him."

¹⁰But God has revealed them to us by His Spirit. For the Spirit searches all things, yes, the deep things of God.

¹¹For what man knows the things of a man, except the spirit of man which is in him? Likewise, no one knows the things of God, except the Spirit of God.

¹²Now we have received not the spirit of the world, but the Spirit which is of God, so that we might know the things that are freely given to us by God.

[13]These things also we proclaim, not in the words which man's wisdom teaches, but which the Holy Spirit teaches, comparing spiritual things with spiritual.

[14]But the natural man does not receive the things of the Spirit of God, for they are foolishness to him; nor can he know them, because they are spiritually discerned.

[15]But he who is spiritual judges all things. Yet he himself is not judged by anyone.

[16]For "who has known the mind of the Lord that he may instruct Him?" But we have the mind of Christ.

DISCUSSION

When spending time in prayer, do you ever not know how to pray for a situation? How does the Holy Spirit help us in these times of prayer? Have you ever seen an attorney plead a case before a judge, either in person or on the television? The Holy Spirit pleads for and represents us before Jesus and the Father. Why do you think this is important? What are your weaknesses? God understands what is going on in your heart. Does it comfort you to know that He understands your anguish over the concerns of your life? Describe your thoughts.

How does God reveal Himself or His will to us? If God's revelation comes through the Holy Spirit and the Holy Spirit searches all things, what should your relationship in prayer with the Holy Spirit be? The Holy Spirit reveals the hidden things of God. Can you receive from God if operating in a worldly mindset? If not, why not? If you want to know the heart and mind of God, then the Holy Spirit has to help you understand. Is it possible for the unspiritual man to consider the things of God? What does the unspiritual man think about the things of God? What does it mean to have the mind of Christ? Is it possible to have the mind of Christ?

Study Notes

_____

_____

_____

_____

_____

C. Evidence that the Holy Spirit Is in Our Lives:

Read Ezekiel 36:26, 27 (NKJV)

I will give you a new heart and put a new spirit within you; I will take the heart of stone out of your flesh and give you a heart of flesh.

²⁷*I will put My Spirit within you and cause you to walk in My statutes, and you will keep My judgments and do them.*

Read John 7:38, 39 (AMP)

He who believes in Me [who cleaves to and trusts in and relies on Me] as the Scripture has said, From his innermost being shall flow [continuously] springs and rivers of living water.

³⁹*But He was speaking here of the Spirit, Whom those who believed (trusted, had faith) in Him were afterward to receive. For the [Holy] Spirit had not yet been given, because Jesus was not yet glorified (raised to honor).*

Read John 15:5 (AMP)

I am the Vine; you are the branches. Whoever lives in Me and I in him bears much (abundant) fruit. However, apart from Me [cut off from vital union with Me] you can do nothing.

Read 2 Corinthians 3:18 (AMP)

And all of us, as with unveiled face, [because we] continued to behold [in the Word of God] as in a mirror the glory of the Lord, are constantly being transfigured into His very own image in ever increasing splendor and from one degree of glory to another; [for this comes] from the Lord [Who is] the Spirit.

Read Galatians 5:16-26 (TLB)

I advise you to obey only the Holy Spirit's instructions. He will tell you where to go and what to do, and then you won't always be doing the wrong things your evil nature wants you to.

¹⁷*For we naturally love to do evil things that are just the opposite from the things that the Holy Spirit tells us to do; and the good things we want to do when the Spirit has his way with us are just the opposite of our natural desires. These two forces within us are constantly fighting each other to win control over us, and our wishes are never free from their pressures.*

¹⁸*When you are guided by the Holy Spirit, you need no longer force yourself to obey Jewish laws.*

¹⁹*But when you follow your own wrong inclinations, your lives will produce these evil results: impure thoughts, eagerness for lustful pleasure,*

²⁰*idolatry, spiritism (that is, encouraging the activity of demons), hatred and fighting, jealousy and anger, constant effort to get the best for yourself, complaints and criticisms, the feeling that everyone else is wrong except those in your own little group—and there will be wrong doctrine,*

²¹*envy, murder, drunkenness, wild parties, and all that sort of thing. Let me tell you again, as I have before, that anyone living that sort of life will not inherit the Kingdom of God.*

²²But when the Holy Spirit controls our lives he will produce this kind of fruit in us: love, joy, peace, patience, kindness, goodness, faithfulness,

²³gentleness and self-control; and here there is no conflict with Jewish laws.

²⁴Those who belong to Christ have nailed their natural evil desires to his cross and crucified them there.

²⁵If we are living now by the Holy Spirit's power, let us follow the Holy Spirit's leading in every part of our lives.

²⁶Then we won't need to look for honors and popularity, which lead to jealousy and hard feelings.

Read Philippians 4:4-9 (NKJV)

Rejoice in the Lord always. Again I will say, rejoice!

⁵Let your gentleness be known to all men. The Lord is at hand.

⁶Be anxious for nothing, but in everything by prayer and supplication, with thanksgiving, let your requests be made known to God;

⁷and the peace of God, which surpasses all understanding, will guard your hearts and minds through Christ Jesus.

⁸Finally, brethren, whatever things are true, whatever things are noble, whatever things are just, whatever things are pure, whatever things are lovely, whatever things are of good report, if there is any virtue and if there is anything praiseworthy--meditate on these things.

⁹The things which you learned and received and heard and saw in me, these do, and the God of peace will be with you.

DISCUSSION

Describe the difference between a heart of flesh and a heart of stone. How can rivers of living water flow out from our lives? What can we do apart from Jesus? With Jesus, we yield what kind of fruit? Explain abundant fruit in your own words. What does a mirror do? How do you daily reflect? We are not to judge others, but is it all right to be a fruit inspector? What are some of the noted differences in the two kinds of fruit found in the Galatians passage? What inputs, both internal and external, produce evil results or good results?

Should the demeanor, conduct, appearance, or character of your life speak for itself? Why or why not? Should these characteristics be evident as people around us watch our behavior? When they see us, what do they say? What do you think about the following words: "The same   Holy Spirit found flowing through Jesus should also produce evidence of His flowing through us"? Do you think it is possible? How will you let the Holy Spirit help you?

Are you "…constantly being transfigured into His very own image in ever increasing splendor and from one degree of glory to another…"? Share how you are yielding yourself to the process.

Study Notes

_____

_____

_____

_____

_____

D. Empowered by the Holy Spirit:

Read Romans 5:5 (NKJV)

Now hope does not disappoint, because the love of God has been poured out in our hearts by the Holy Spirit who was given to us.

Read 2 Corinthians 3:5, 6 (AMP)

Not that we are fit (qualified and sufficient in ability) of ourselves to form personal judgments or to claim or count anything as coming from us, but our power and ability and sufficiency are from God.

[It is He] Who has qualified us [making us to be fit and worthy and sufficient] as ministers and dispensers of a new covenant [of salvation through Christ], not [ministers] of the letter (of legally written code) but of the Spirit; for the code [of the Law] kills, but the [Holy] Spirit makes alive.

Read Ephesians 1:13, 14 (TLB)

And because of what Christ did, all you others too, who heard the Good News about how to be saved, and trusted Christ, were marked as belonging to Christ by the Holy Spirit, who long ago had been promised to all of us Christians.

His presence within us is God's guarantee that he really will give us all that he promised; and the Spirit's seal upon us means that God has already purchased us and that he guarantees to bring us to himself. This is just one more reason for us to praise our glorious God.

Read Ephesians 1:19, 20 (TLB)

I pray that you will begin to understand how incredibly great his power is to help those who believe him. It is that same mighty power

that raised Christ from the dead and seated him in the place of honor at God's right hand in heaven.

Read 1 Thessalonians 1:5 (NKJV)

For our gospel did not come to you in word only, but also in power, and in the Holy Spirit and in much assurance, as you know what kind of men we were among you for your sake.

DISCUSSION

Summarize these passages in your own words. Share how the power of the Holy Spirit operates in your life. Soak in for a moment the absolute power of God, which is now flowing through you. Remarkable! Remember that God qualifies you for the ministry set before you. He fills in the gaps by inconspicuously (quietly) empowering your life through the indwelling of the Holy Spirit in your life. Does that bring peace to you and calm you? Why? Do you feel overwhelmed from time to time? A sailboat without wind will only sit in the water looking pretty, but with a consistent wind to fill the sails, it will move forward. The Holy Spirit daily empowers our lives to consistently move forward. When we feel insufficient, he suffices. When we don't know what to say, he inspires us to share the good news and hope of what Jesus did for all of the world.

Study Notes

_____

_____

_____

_____

Part 4: One Body and One Spirit; Grieving and Resisting the Holy Spirit

A. One Body and One Holy Spirit

Read 1 Corinthians 12:1-13 (TLB)

And now, brothers, I want to write about the special abilities the Holy Spirit gives to each of you, for I don't want any misunderstanding about them.

²You will remember that before you became Christians you went around from one idol to another, not one of which could speak a single word.

³But now you are meeting people who claim to speak messages from the Spirit of God. How can you know whether they are really inspired by God or whether they are fakes? Here is the test: no one speaking by the power of the Spirit of God can curse Jesus, and no one can say, "Jesus is Lord," and really mean it, unless the Holy Spirit is helping him.

⁴Now God gives us many kinds of special abilities, but it is the same Holy Spirit who is the source of them all.

⁵There are different kinds of service to God, but it is the same Lord we are serving.

⁶There are many ways in which God works in our lives, but it is the same God who does the work in and through all of us who are his.

⁷The Holy Spirit displays God's power through each of us as a means of helping the entire church.

⁸To one person the Spirit gives the ability to give wise advice; someone else may be especially good at studying and teaching, and this is his gift from the same Spirit.

⁹He gives special faith to another, and to someone else the power to heal the sick.

¹⁰He gives power for doing miracles to some, and to others power to prophesy and preach. He gives someone else the power to know whether evil spirits are speaking through those who claim to be giving God's messages—or whether it is really the Spirit of God who is speaking. Still another person is able to speak in languages he never learned; and others, who do not know the language either, are given power to understand what he is saying.

¹¹It is the same and only Holy Spirit who gives all these gifts and powers, deciding which each one of us should have.

¹²Our bodies have many parts, but the many parts make up only one body when they are all put together. So it is with the "body" of Christ.

¹³Each of us is a part of the one body of Christ. Some of us are Jews, some are Gentiles, some are slaves, and some are free. But the Holy Spirit has fitted us all together into one body. We have been baptized into Christ's body by the one Spirit, and have all been given that same Holy Spirit.

DISCUSSION

Where do our abilities come from? How can we test if a person's spirit is from God or not? What are the different ways the Holy Spirit operates in the body of Christ? Do you own your gift from God? Why or why not? Is there one gift or operation in the body of Christ that is more important than another? Why do you think there are so many different parts and distributions of the gifts? How should you play your part in the body of Christ? Do you look at the other members of the body of Christ as your equals?

The body of Christ is like a puzzle; we all are a piece of the puzzle. Each of us has to play our part. We shouldn't want to be someone else's piece. If you are envious of another's part, you are saying to God that what He has asked you to do isn't good enough. You are displaying discontentment, and you will lose your peace. Your ministry is enough. Are you sharing Christ where you are being asked to serve?

Study Notes

_____

_____

_____

_____

_____

B. Resisting the Holy Spirit

Read Matthew 12:31, 32 (AMP)

Therefore I tell you, every sin and blasphemy (every evil, abusive, injurious speaking, or indignity against sacred things) can be forgiven men, but blasphemy against the [Holy] Spirit shall not and cannot be forgiven.

[32] And whoever speaks a word against the Son of Man will be forgiven, but whoever speaks against the Spirit, the Holy One, will not be forgiven, either in this world and age or in the world and age to come.

Read Acts 7:48-52 (MEV)

"However, the Most High does not dwell in houses made with hands. As the prophet says:

[49] 'Heaven is My throne, and the earth is My footstool. What house will you build for Me? says the Lord, or what is the place of My rest?

[50] Has not My hand made all these things?'

[51] "You stiff-necked people, uncircumcised in heart and ears! You always resist the Holy Spirit. As your fathers did, so do you.

[52] Which of the prophets have your fathers not persecuted? They have even killed those who fore-told the coming of the Righteous One, of whom you have now become the betrayers and murderers,

Read Hebrews 10:26-31 (TLB)

If anyone sins deliberately by rejecting the Savior after knowing the truth of forgiveness, this sin is not covered by Christ's death; there is no way to get rid of it.

[27] There will be nothing to look forward to but the terrible punishment of God's awful anger, which will consume all his enemies.

[28] A man who refused to obey the laws given by Moses was killed without mercy if there were two or three witnesses to his sin.

[29] Think how much more terrible the punishment will be for those who have trampled underfoot

the Son of God and treated his cleansing blood as though it were common and unhallowed, and insulted and outraged the Holy Spirit who brings God's mercy to his people.

30For we know him who said, "Justice belongs to me; I will repay them"; who also said, "The Lord himself will handle these cases."

31It is a fearful thing to fall into the hands of the living God.

DISCUSSION

Our humanity can cause us to be very closed-off, self-sufficient, self-absorbed, and disregarding of others, often spending our days as if there is no need for anyone else. What is blaspheming the Holy Spirit? Why do you think blaspheming against the Holy Spirit is warned against? Does this seem unfair to you? Why is there such a severe consequence? Why do you think there is so much importance placed on honoring and respecting the Holy Spirit? Describe in your words what it means to be "stiff necked and uncircumcised in heart and ears." Have you ever resisted the Holy Spirit? Can you share an experience when you did and what you learned from it?

Have you ever considered someone's coming to Christ, being forgiven for their sins, and then turning away from Jesus? Is it possible? How does a person get to this place in his life? What must be the condition of his heart? Those who treat the blood of Christ as if it were common cause outrage, offense, and anger to the Holy Spirit. How do we treat something as common? Do you think the Holy Spirit will be merciful? Can you give some examples of those who have fallen into the hands of God when He was angry? It is scary—very scary—to consider being so insolent (disrespectful)!

Study Notes

C. Grieving the Holy Spirit

Read Isaiah 63:9, 10 (NKJV)

In all their affliction He was afflicted, And the Angel of His Presence saved them; In His love and in His pity He redeemed them; And He bore them and carried them All the days of old.

¹⁰But they rebelled and grieved His Holy Spirit; So He turned Himself against them as an enemy, And He fought against them.

Read Ephesians 4:17 (NKJV)

This I say, therefore, and testify in the Lord, that you should no longer walk as the rest of the Gentiles walk, in the futility of their mind.

Read Ephesians 4:30-32 (NKJV)

And do not grieve the Holy Spirit of God, by whom you were sealed for the day of redemption.

³¹Let all bitterness, wrath, anger, clamor, and evil speaking be put away from you, with all malice.

³²And be kind to one another, tenderhearted, forgiving one another, just as God in Christ forgave you.

Read 2 Timothy 3:1-5 (NKJV)

But know this, that in the last days perilous times will come:

²For men will be lovers of themselves, lovers of money, boasters, proud, blasphemers, disobedient to parents, unthankful, unholy,

³unloving, unforgiving, slanderers, without self-control, brutal, despisers of good,

⁴traitors, headstrong, haughty, lovers of pleasure rather than lovers of God,

⁵having a form of godliness but denying its power. And from such people turn away!

Read 1 Thessalonians 5:19 (NKJV)

¹⁹Do not quench the Spirit.

DISCUSSION

When you grieve, your heart is broken. Depending on what you are grieved over, it may take a very long time for you to be consoled or comforted. Our actions (choices that we make) matter because they reflect the condition of our heart and what we value in our life.

How would you feel if God turned and fought against you? What does it means to "walk in the futility of their mind"? Does our behavior grieve the Holy Spirit? How? The passage in 2 Timothy

3:1-5 is not written to the ungodly community but is addressed to the Christians in Ephesus. Note that these behaviors were concerns for the believers. How would such behaviors grieve the Holy Spirit?

Does your attitude deny or embrace the Holy Spirit in your life? Who or what groups influence your life and shape your thoughts toward the Holy Spirit? Finally, how does a Christian *"...quench the Spirit"*?

Study Notes

_____

_____

_____

_____

Application: The importance of the Holy Spirit can't be emphasized enough. He is just that significant in our daily life. He fulfills the Trinity of God. At this time on the biblical calendar, the Holy Spirit empowers, guides, teaches, and gives us access to the thoughts, will, and purposes of God the Father through Jesus the Son. Jesus referred to the **Holy Spirit** as coming after Him. It is through the Holy Spirit of God that you are able to have the daily strength to walk out your Christian life. It is the Holy Spirit Who directs, instructs, and reveals to you how to daily walk out your Christian life. The Spirit of God makes the Word of God clear as you read it. The Holy Spirit of God is active and moving among people, drawing them into relationship with God. He helps us proclaim Jesus and edify those around us every day. The Holy Spirit cleanses, purifies, and pours over your life, changing your heart (attitudes and motives), thoughts, desires, and spirit, making them brand new and recreated. The Holy Spirit is the power of Heaven living through your life on a daily basis! Let go and release control of your life, completely trusting the guidance and direction given to you from the Holy Spirit.

Going a step deeper, we understand the Holy Spirit's role to guide us in our life choices. Those choices can impact your daily or long-term choices and your destiny. As your relationship with the Holy Spirit grows and deepens, so does your confidence in the guidance of the Holy Spirit. You develop a conviction or a firmness of belief that you are making the right decision. When you go outside the will of God for your life or start heading down a direction that is not best for you, the Holy Spirit convicts you of your bad decision as a means of giving you direction. When you make very wrong decisions that are clear violations of God's best for your life, you are sinning (rebelling) against the will of God as found in the Scriptures. So it is important to cultivate a sensitivity to the

Holy Spirit (also known as walking with the Holy Spirit). Walking with the Holy Spirit restrains you from making sinful choices; this relationship reveals God's forgiveness during repentance when you are convicted of sinful choices; it encourages, strengthens, and gives a sense of peace when you show self-control and do what is right.

Daily walk with the Holy Spirit as you make the choices that come to you each day. The Holy Spirit is the Comforter. You are not alone and don't have to walk by yourself. Every task and decision presented to you is important and not without merit before God.

For every person who receives Jesus Christ as Savior, the indwelling presence of the Holy Spirit gives a ministry gift to be used to edify (build up) and encourage the body of Christ. Every believer should be encouraged to seek the gift the Holy Spirit has given him. This can be done by prayer, asking the Holy Spirit to reveal that gift or those gifts. Inventories to help you discover your spiritual gifts are available. Ask your pastor for his recommendation concerning a specific inventory and ask your pastor and friends what they see in you as your special ministry gift. Once determined, this gift or these gifts are to be used in the life of the church for instruction and encouragement and to edify or build up the spiritual health of the local church.

The Holy Spirit helps you fulfill Jesus' instruction to proclaim the gospel to all the world. He enables you to be more like Jesus, to take on His character and attributes. He transforms you to be like Jesus. Plus, Jesus said that believers would do greater works than He did, but they can't do them without the help of the Holy Spirit. Life is all about Jesus and glorifying Him, but you can't do these greater works on your own. That is why you need the help of the Holy Spirit in your life.

Final Thoughts

Proverbs 29:23   If you are humble in spirit, then you retain honor.
Proverbs 16:18   If you have a haughty spirit, then it results in a fall.
Psalm 34:18   If you have a broken and contrite spirit, the Lord is near you.

Further Study

Psalm 51:11, 12; 139:7 Isaiah 61:1-3; 66:13 Jeremiah 31:33
Ezekiel 11-19; 36:25-27 Zechariah 12:10 Matthew 10:19, 20
Mark 16:17, 18 Luke 1:15, 41, 67; 4:8; 11:1-13 Luke 18:1-8; 24:49
John 3:3-6; 14:21; 16:7-14 Acts 1:8; 4:8, 31; 6:3, 5 Acts 7:55; 11:15
Romans 5:5; 6:4; 8:1-17, 26, 27 1 Corinthians 2:9-16, 6:19 I Corinthians chapter 12
2 Corinthians 13:5 Galatians 2:20; 3:1-5, 28 Galatians 4:6, 7; 5:18; 6:8
Ephesians 1:3 (AMP) Ephesians 2:1-3; 3:14-19 (AMP) Colossians 1:21, 27
2 Timothy 1:7 Titus 3:5 Hebrews 3:1-19
1 John 1:7; 2:20-27

Notes

"The Lord is a warrior..."
Exodus 15:3 (NET)

Part 2: The Warrior Ring

Lesson 4
Producing Fruit in Our Lives

JESUS NEVER DID ANYTHING that He did not see His Father doing. The fruit produced in His life was a result of His obedience. That obedience glorified the Father. We too can do nothing in our own ability or strength. It is only through and with the Holy Spirit that we produce any kind of fruit in our lives. The Holy Spirit is in direct communion with the Father and the Son, so He knows how best to act in our life. Through us the Holy Spirit is manifested, and His purpose is to glorify and reflect Jesus. Only by staying connected to the vine (Jesus) and energized by the Holy Spirit can we gain fruitfulness.

John 15:1 (NKJV) says Jesus is "the true vine, and My Father is the vinedresser." It's the vinedresser I want to focus on for a moment. A vinedresser is a master gardener that tends and prunes grapevines. The master knows how to prune, how much to cut, how far back to cut, and where the vine needs to be pruned. He sees the why in each cut because it is for the purpose of producing maximum fruitfulness on each vine under his care. The Father (the Gardener) expects a result from watering, cultivating, weeding, and pruning. We don't need to know why, but we do need to trust the Master. Through eyes of love, He sees all of your potential, and He knows how to bring it out in your life. Jesus said that He could do nothing apart from the Holy Spirit; you can't either.

Producing fruit in your life is a process. It can't be academic or just something you know. It has to be produced through experience with Jesus and the Holy Spirit, resulting in wisdom, discernment, and understanding. Much like character, you either have it or you don't. Now you can be somewhere in between the process of getting it and having it on any given day. Some days you may be more successful in reflecting Jesus' character, as evidenced by your visible fruitfulness. The fruits of the Spirit found in Galatians 5:22-23, as an illustration, are love, joy, peace, longsuffering, kindness, goodness, faithfulness, gentleness, and self-control.

Other places in the Scripture provide more examples, but let's focus on the ones found in

Galatians. Just nine separate fruits are in this list, but wow! Can you say you have all of them in your life? One day you might have five of the nine or another day eight of the nine; then the next day you might have only three of the nine. Producing fruit isn't easy; it's very difficult. Unless you submit to the help of the Holy Spirit, it's impossible to produce fruit.

Let me demonstrate my point. While I was driving to a scheduled military training event, my vehicle had a flat tire. When I pulled over and confirmed that it was indeed a flat tire, I said to myself, No big deal. I've got emergency roadside service through my vehicle insurance company. This should only take about an hour to fix, and then I can be on my way. I called the insurance claim agent, and after being on the phone with him for almost thirty minutes, he said that it would be forty-five to sixty minutes before someone would be able to assist me. I said to myself, Okay, I'll only be about fifteen minutes off of my original estimation. I still had time to make it to my training event, even if it took the extra fifteen minutes.

While I was waiting for assistance, the state police stopped and asked me if I was all right and if I needed any assistance. I told them that I was waiting for the roadside service and that they would be there in about fifteen minutes. They gave me contact information in case I needed help and left. Almost two hours after my call for help, patience was needed; I wasn't doing very well. My patience with the situation was stretched, and I was starting to feel frustrated. After two and a half hours, I called the state police back. They sent out a patrol car to assist. When the police arrived, it took me five minutes to change my tire and be on my way.

It wasn't a good day for someone to observe my patience meter. Patience was low, and I had to ask the Lord for forgiveness for letting the circumstances get to me. But this is just one illustration of how the fruit of the Spirit must be grown in our lives. You can't just say, "I have patience." It has to be demonstrated consistently in our lives. You never know when a particular fruit will be tested in your life. But you can yield yourself to the daily molding of your life so that you will reflect more of Jesus. Pressures reveal what real fruit is inside.

Our lives are expected to be fruitful, which also means being productive, profitable, and successful. In Genesis 1:28, God the Father told Adam and Eve to be fruitful and multiply. He didn't say to be a failure or fruitless (unproductive). Every seed planted in the ground is carefully cultivated to multiply. God has planted His seed within each and every one of us. That seed has all of the nature and characteristics of Who God is and Who we will become. The manifestation of the fruit of the Spirit is germinating in each of us. God does a complete work.

Read John 15:1-8 (MEV)

"I am the true vine, and My Father is the vinedresser.

²Every branch in Me that bears no fruit, He takes away. And every branch that bears fruit, He prunes, that it may bear more fruit.

³You are already clean through the word which I have spoken to you.

⁴Remain in Me, as I also remain in you. As the branch cannot bear fruit by itself, unless it remains in the vine, neither can you, unless you remain in Me.

⁵"I am the vine, you are the branches. He who remains in Me, and I in him, bears much fruit. For without Me you can do nothing.

⁶If a man does not remain in Me, he is thrown out as a branch and withers. And they gather them and throw them into the fire, and they are burned.

⁷If you remain in Me, and My words remain in you, you will ask whatever you desire, and it shall be done for you.

⁸My Father is glorified by this, that you bear much fruit; so you will be My disciples.

DISCUSSION

How would you describe fruitfulness? What are some of the evidences of it? How do you stay connected to the vine (Jesus)? What does it mean to you that Jesus is the root?

Vs. 2   What does pruning look like in your life? Who is doing the pruning? What should be your attitude toward pruning?

Vs. 4   How does it make you feel when this verse says you can't bear your own fruit?

Vs. 6   Is it harsh that some are cast out? What should your life reflect?

Vs. 8   What is the Father's desire and why?

Study Notes

_____

_____

_____

_____

_____

Read John 15:4, 5 (MEV)

Remain in Me, as I also remain in you. As the branch cannot bear fruit by itself, unless it remains in the vine, neither can you, unless you remain in Me.

⁵"I am the vine, you are the branches. He who remains in Me, and I in him, bears much fruit. For without Me you can do nothing.

Read Mark 4:3-8 (NKJV)

"Listen! Behold, a sower went out to sow

⁴And it happened, as he sowed, that some seed fell by the wayside; and the birds of the air came and devoured it.

⁵Some fell on stony ground, where it did not have much earth; and immediately it sprang up because it had no depth of earth.

⁶But when the sun was up it was scorched, and because it had no root it withered away.

⁷And some seed fell among thorns; and the thorns grew up and choked it, and it yielded no crop.

⁸But other seed fell on good ground and yielded a crop that sprang up, increased and produced: some thirtyfold, some sixty, and some a hundred."

Read Mark 4:14-20 (NKJV)

The sower sows the word.

¹⁵And these are the ones by the wayside where the word is sown. When they hear, Satan comes immediately and takes away the word that was sown in their hearts.

¹⁶These likewise are the ones sown on stony ground who, when they hear the word, immediately receive it with gladness;

¹⁷and they have no root in themselves, and so endure only for a time. Afterward, when tribulation or persecution arises for the word's sake, immediately they stumble.

¹⁸Now these are the ones sown among thorns; they are the ones who hear the word,

¹⁹and the cares of this world, the deceitfulness of riches, and the desires for other things entering in choke the word, and it becomes unfruitful.

²⁰But these are the ones sown on good ground, those who hear the word, accept it, and bear fruit: some thirtyfold, some sixty, and some a hundred."

DISCUSSION

Let's look a little deeper into these verses. Anything that has fruitfulness is a result of careful cultivation. According to John 15:4-5, what is your responsibility? Can you do anything for yourself apart from Jesus? What kind of fruit do you produce apart from Jesus? Describe the four situations (types of ground) that the seed fell on, as listed in Mark 4:3-8, and the results.

Compare verses 14-20 with verses 3-8. What do you see? What "cares of the world" often choke out and compete with your growth and fruitfulness? Why do you think there are different increases: thirty, sixty, and a hundred? Do you think that's fair? Why or why not?

Study Notes

_____

_____

_____

_____

_____

Types of Fruit

Normally when talking about the fruitfulness of a person's life, the words are referring to the external manifestations of an internal relationship either with or without the Holy Spirit. When the effort is your own, one type of result is manifested, and when you are yielded to the influence of the Holy Spirit, a different result is manifested.

A. Works of the Flesh (Unfruitfulness/Selfishness)

Read Galatians 5:19-21 (NKJV)

Now the works of the flesh are evident, which are: adultery, fornication, uncleanness, lewdness,
[20]idolatry, sorcery, hatred, contentions, jealousies, outbursts of wrath, selfish ambitions, dissensions, heresies,
[21]envy, murders, drunkenness, revelries, and the like; of which I tell you beforehand, just as I also told you in time past, that those who practice such things will not inherit the kingdom of God.

Read Ephesians 4:30, 31 (NKJV)

And do not grieve the Holy Spirit of God, by whom you were sealed for the day of redemption.
[31]Let all bitterness, wrath, anger, clamor, and evil speaking be put away from you, with all malice.

Read Ephesians 5:3-5 (NKJV)

But fornication and all uncleanness or covetousness, let it not even be named among you, as is fitting for saints;
[4]neither filthiness, nor foolish talking, nor coarse jesting, which are not fitting, but rather giving of thanks.
[5]For this you know, that no fornicator, unclean person, nor covetous man, who is an idolater, has any inheritance in the kingdom of Christ and God.

Read Jude 1:18, 19 (NKJV)

>   how they told you that there would be mockers in the last time who would walk according to their own ungodly lusts.
>
>   ¹⁹These are sensual persons, who cause divisions, not having the Spirit.

B. Works of the Spirit (Fruitfulness/Selflessness)

Read Galatians 5:22, 23 (NKJV)

>   But the fruit of the Spirit is love, joy, peace, longsuffering, kindness, goodness, faithfulness,
>   ²³gentleness, self-control. Against such there is no law.

Read Ephesians 4:32 (NKJV)

>   And be kind to one another, tenderhearted, forgiving one another, just as God in Christ forgave you.

Read Ephesians 5:1, 2 (NKJV)

>   Therefore be imitators of God as dear children.
>   ²³And walk in love, as Christ also has loved us and given Himself for us, an offering and a sacrifice to God for a sweet-smelling aroma.

Read Ephesians 5:9 (NKJV)

>   (for the fruit of the Spirit is in all goodness, righteousness, and truth),

Read 2 Peter 1:5-9 (NKJV)

>   But also for this very reason, giving all diligence, add to your faith virtue, to virtue knowledge,
>   ⁶to knowledge self-control, to self-control perseverance, to perseverance godliness,
>   ⁷to godliness brotherly kindness, and to brotherly kindness love.
>   ⁸For if these things are yours and abound, you will be neither barren nor unfruitful in the knowledge of our Lord Jesus Christ.
>   ⁹For he who lacks these things is shortsighted, even to blindness, and has forgotten that he was cleansed from his old sins.

Read 1 John 2:10 (NKJV)

>   He who loves his brother abides in the light, and there is no cause for stumbling in him.

DISCUSSION

What observations can you make to distinguish the differences between these two types of fruitfulness or character traits? Are there promises (blessings or curses) associated with either? What are they?

Study Notes

_____

_____

_____

_____

_____

What Types of Fruit Are You Bearing?

Read John 12:24-26 (NKJV)

Most assuredly, I say to you, unless a grain of wheat falls into the ground and dies, it remains alone; but if it dies, it produces much grain.

²⁵He who loves his life will lose it, and he who hates his life in this world will keep it for eternal life.

²⁶If anyone serves Me, let him follow Me; and where I am, there My servant will be also. If anyone serves Me, him My Father will honor.

Read Luke 3:8, 9 (NKJV)

"Therefore bear fruits worthy of repentance, and do not begin to say to yourselves, 'We have Abraham as our father.' For I say to you that God is able to raise up children to Abraham from these stones.

⁹And even now the ax is laid to the root of the trees. Therefore every tree which does not bear good fruit is cut down and thrown into the fire."

Read Luke 6:43-45 (NKJV)

"For a good tree does not bear bad fruit, nor does a bad tree bear good fruit.

⁴⁴For every tree is known by its own fruit. For men do not gather figs from thorns, nor do they gather grapes from a bramble bush.

⁴⁵A good man out of the good treasure of his heart brings forth good; and an evil man out of the evil treasure of his heart brings forth evil. For out of the abundance of the heart his mouth speaks.

Read Luke 13:6-9 (NKJV)

He also spoke this parable: "A certain man had a fig tree planted in his vineyard, and he came seeking fruit on it and found none.

Then he said to the keeper of his vineyard, 'Look, for three years I have come seeking fruit on this fig tree and find none. Cut it down; why does it use up the ground?'

8But he answered and said to him, 'Sir, let it alone this year also, until I dig around it and fertilize it.

9And if it bears fruit, well. But if not, after that you can cut it down.' "

Read Romans 6:22 (NKJV)

But now having been set free from sin, and having become slaves of God, you have your fruit to holiness, and the end, everlasting life.

Read Galatians 6:7-9 (NKJV)

Do not be deceived, God is not mocked; for whatever a man sows, that he will also reap.

8For he who sows to his flesh will of the flesh reap corruption, but he who sows to the Spirit will of the Spirit reap everlasting life.

9And let us not grow weary while doing good, for in due season we shall reap if we do not lose heart.

Read Ephesians 5:8-13 (NKJV)

For you were once darkness, but now you are light in the Lord. Walk as children of light

9(for the fruit of the Spirit is in all goodness, righteousness, and truth),

10finding out what is acceptable to the Lord.

11And have no fellowship with the unfruitful works of darkness, but rather expose them.

12For it is shameful even to speak of those things which are done by them in secret.

13But all things that are exposed are made manifest by the light, for whatever makes manifest is light.

Read Ephesians 5:15-21 (NKJV)

See then that you walk circumspectly, not as fools but as wise,

16redeeming the time, because the days are evil.

17Therefore do not be unwise, but understand what the will of the Lord is.

18And do not be drunk with wine, in which is dissipation; but be filled with the Spirit,

19speaking to one another in psalms and hymns and spiritual songs, singing and making melody in your heart to the Lord,

²⁰giving thanks always for all things to God the Father in the name of our Lord Jesus Christ,
²¹submitting to one another in the fear of God.

Read 1 John 2:6 (NKJV)

He who says he abides in Him ought himself also to walk just as He walked.

DISCUSSION

In order for you to bear fruit, how should you look at your life? What causes you not to bear fruit? What happens to the life that doesn't bear fruit? What is that difference? What part does the attitude of your heart play in the bearing of fruit in your life? Do you think God is patient with the process of fruit production in our lives? Why do you think that? Share your thoughts about sowing and reaping. Why do you think God expects your life to change? Why do you think others will expect your life to change? Can you ever really get away with doing anything secretly? What does walking circumspectly mean to you?

Study Notes

_____

_____

_____

_____

_____

Examining the Fruit

The nine individual fruits or character traits listed in Galatians 5:22 and 23 are connected and form a foundation in our lives. They exemplify who Christ is and reflect the Father, enabled in our lives by the Holy Spirit.

Read Galatians 5:22, 23 (NKJV)

But the fruit of the Spirit is love, joy, peace, longsuffering, kindness, goodness, faithfulness,
²³gentleness, self-control. Against such there is no law.

Define *love, joy, peace, longsuffering, kindness, goodness, faithfulness, gentleness,* and *self-control.*

_____

_____

_____

_____

_____

_____

_____

Describe *love, joy, peace, longsuffering, kindness, goodness, faithfulness, gentleness, self-control.*

_____

_____

_____

_____

_____

_____

_____

_____

Give an example of *love, joy, peace, longsuffering, kindness, goodness, faithfulness, gentleness, self-control.*

_____

_____

_____

_____

_____

_____

_____

Read 1 Corinthians 13:4-8 (TLB)

Love is very patient and kind, never jealous or envious, never boastful or proud,

⁵never haughty or selfish or rude. Love does not demand its own way. It is not irritable or touchy. It does not hold grudges and will hardly even notice when others do it wrong.

⁶It is never glad about injustice, but rejoices whenever truth wins out.

⁷If you love someone, you will be loyal to him no matter what the cost. You will always believe in him, always expect the best of him, and always stand your ground in defending him.

⁸All the special gifts and powers from God will someday come to an end, but love goes on forever. Someday prophecy and speaking in unknown languages and special knowledge—these gifts will disappear.

Love

Love is a verb in both the Galatians and 1 Corinthians passages listed above. It is an action!

Joy (Gladness)

Joy is a noun. Synonyms for joy are delight, happiness, pleasure, bliss, contentment, ecstasy, and elation.

Read Nehemiah 8:10 (NKJV)

it is a time to celebrate with a hearty meal and to send presents to those in need, for the joy of the Lord is your strength. You must not be dejected and sad!"

Peace

Peace reflects harmony, quietness, and serenity. It means "free from anxiety or anxiousness; no conflict or disagreement."

Read James 3:18 (NKJV)

Now the fruit of righteousness is sown in peace by those who make peace.

Longsuffering (Patience or Even Temperament)

The Encarta dictionary says *longsuffering* is "patience and endurance in the face of suffering or difficulty." Some synonyms are *tolerance, patience,* or *selflessness.*

Read 2 Peter 3:9 (NKJV)

The Lord is not slack concerning His promise, as some count slackness, but is longsuffering toward us, not willing that any should perish but that all should come to repentance.

Kindness (Gentleness)

Kindness means "goodness of heart." Encarta says *kindness* is "the practice of being or the tendency to be sympathetic and compassionate." Some synonyms are *compassion, sympathy, kindheartedness, thoughtfulness,* and *consideration.*

Read Ephesians 2:7 (TLB)

And now God can always point to us as examples of how very, very rich his kindness is, as shown in all he has done for us through Jesus Christ.

Goodness

The word *goodness* signifies a moral quality. Synonyms are *integrity, honesty,* and *decency.*

Read 2 Thessalonians 1:11 (NKJV)

Therefore we also pray always for you that our God would count you worthy of this calling, and fulfill all the good pleasure of His goodness and the work of faith with power,

Faithfulness (Faith)

Faith signifies an assurance in something or a conviction.

Read 1 Corinthians 15:14-17 (NKJV)

And if Christ is not risen, then our preaching is empty and your faith is also empty.
[15]Yes, and we are found false witnesses of God, because we have testified of God that He raised up Christ, whom He did not raise up--if in fact the dead do not rise.
[16]For if the dead do not rise, then Christ is not risen.
[17]And if Christ is not risen, your faith is futile; you are still in your sins!

Gentleness (Meekness)

Synonyms for *gentleness* are *mildness, calmness, tenderness,* and *quietness.* Humility is implied in this word.

Read Matthew 5:5 (NKJV)

Blessed are the meek, For they shall inherit the earth.

Self-Control (Temperance)

Self-control indicates the idea of restraint.

Read 1 Corinthians 9:24-27 (NKJV)

Do you not know that those who run in a race all run, but one receives the prize? Run in such a way that you may obtain it.

²⁵And everyone who competes for the prize is temperate in all things. Now they do it to obtain a perishable crown, but we for an imperishable crown.

²⁶Therefore I run thus: not with uncertainty. Thus I fight: not as one who beats the air.

²⁷But I discipline my body and bring it into subjection, lest, when I have preached to others, I myself should become disqualified.

Read Psalm 1:1-3 (NKJV)

Blessed is the man Who walks not in the counsel of the ungodly, Nor stands in the path of sinners, Nor sits in the seat of the scornful;

²But his delight is in the law of the LORD, And in His law he meditates day and night.

³He shall be like a tree Planted by the rivers of water, That brings forth its fruit in its season, Whose leaf also shall not wither; And whatever he does shall prosper.

DISCUSSION

Matthew 7:13-20. The way to life is narrow. Do you think it's unfair that the way to God is narrow? Can you always tell what's in a person's life just by looking at their outer appearance? What should you be looking for?

Study Notes

_____

_____

_____

_____

_____

Application: The Bible enumerates the fruit of the Holy Spirit in Galatians 5:22-23: love, joy, peace, longsuffering, kindness, goodness, faithfulness, gentleness, and self-control. The Spirit reproduces these virtues in the life of the believer. A Christian who has been regenerated by the Holy Spirit and in whom the Spirit dwells can expect to develop a lifestyle in response to the Spirit's motivation. The gifts of the Spirit pertain to witness and service; the fruit of the Spirit pertain to the believer's character. The fruit of the Spirit is the harvest that results when a life is lived in submission to the Spirit.

Paul gives these virtues in his letter to the Galatians. In a similar passage, Peter instructs the believer to *"make every effort to add to your faith, goodness; and to goodness, knowledge; and to knowledge, self-control; and to self-control, perseverance; and to perseverance, godliness; and to godliness, mutual affection; and to mutual affection, love.* — 2 Peter 1:5-7 (NIV) God is concerned that His people display traits of character that complement the Holy Spirit Who dwells with the Christian.

Fruitfulness is interesting because it reflects the outward appearance of the inward character possessed by the individual. This character is manifested so all can see its actions and moral fiber in motion. The expectation is that our life will bear fruit! Jesus in His relationship with His Father yielded Himself, acknowledging that He Himself was the vine and His Father was the gardener. We too have no control over our fruitfulness; if we stay connected to Jesus, He is the vine and we are the branch. He determines our fruitfulness, and our job is to stay connected to the branch. Many would say that we should not judge another person, with which I agree. But whether one has a fruitful life or not should be evident to those who are observing the notable character differences exhibited in the daily lives of individuals.

The fruit is what others see outwardly of what is going on internally in our lives. It is not our responsibility to determine how much fruit is in our lives. We are just to abide in and on the vine (Jesus). The fruit in our lives is determined by someone else: God the Father. Our fruitfulness is not achieved through our own efforts, but through God's grace and mercy. There is a plan and a purpose for each of our lives, and whatever that is will be reflected in the fruit in our lives. Our lives are cared for and tended to (pruned) so they will reflect the joy and peace of being in relationship with God. The reflection of that fruit comes forth in our lives as others notice love, joy, peace, patience, gentleness, and self-control in our lives. The observation of notable change is what draws others to our lives as we are committed to Jesus.

Note: Again, you must respond to God's influence. If your life is truly yielded to the power of the Holy Spirit, then it will reflect that desired change. Selflessness is expressed through changed outward evidences of behaviors, lifestyle choices, relationships with others, and overall countenance. How you respond to God will determine what type of fruit your life will produce: a god-like, others-focused lifestyle or a god-less, self-centered, worldly lifestyle. Your life will not change overnight, but it won't change at all unless you yield yourself to the transforming work of the Holy Spirit. You have to stay connected to become like Jesus.

Further Study
Fruitfulness

Job 8:11-13	Psalms 1:1-3; 92:13, 14	Isaiah 5:1-7
Jeremiah 17:7, 8	Matthew 13:8, 23; 15:13-20; 21:33	John 8:31; 12:24; 15:10, 18
Romans 5:3, 4; 6:22; 7:4	2 Corinthians 3:5; 9:6-10	Galatians 5:16, 17, 18, 21, 22-26

Ephesians 5:9, 11   Philippians 1:9-11, 22   Philippians 2:3, 4, 14, 15

Philippians 4:8, 9, 17   Colossians 1:9-14; 3:8-17; 4:6   2 Peter 1:2-9, 22

Hebrews 12:11   James 3:17   1 John 4:15; 2:6, 10, 24

I John 3:6, 24; 5:20   2 John 1:9

Unfruitfulness

Proverbs 10:16; 13:2   Hosea 10:13; 3:11   Matthew 3:10; 7:17, 18

Matthew 12:33;13:4, 22   Matthew 15:19; 21:19; 25:25   Romans 7:5

Galatians 5:19-21   James 1:5

Recommended Reading: *Abiding in Christ* by Andrew Murray

Notes

_____

_____

_____

_____

_____

_____

_____

_____

_____

_____

_____

_____

_____

_____

_____

_____

_____

_____

"The Lord is a warrior..."
Exodus 15:3 (NET)

Part 2: The Warrior Ring

Lesson 5
Daily Vigilance
(The Full Armor of God)

WITHIN ALL MEN, there is a desire to be a part of a purpose larger than themselves. That purpose has to be honorable and full of integrity in order to draw men to it. They have to feel their contribution is worth the sacrifice made so that they can justify the role they will play in its success. Men will ask questions such as the following: Will it make a difference or an impact? What if I don't do a thing? Will it matter? Will others benefit from my contribution? Is this calling or purpose worth my time? Is it worth dying for if required? You are being called to be a warrior for God or a man after God's own heart.

You have been called to follow Jesus. Jesus said in **Matthew 16:24** (NKJV), "If anyone desires to come after Me, let him deny himself, and take up his cross, and follow Me." You are being called to be a disciple (warrior). A disciple (warrior) of Jesus follows and accepts His teachings and strives to be like the Master, pursuing with all their ability and denying themselves to be like Jesus. **Luke 6:40** (NKJV) says, *"A disciple is not above his teacher, but everyone who is perfectly trained will be like his teacher."* Jesus didn't just call his disciples; He trained them and poured his heart and soul into them, equipping them for what challenges awaited them.

As the Master, He knew what His disciples would face. He knew how to individually groom each of the disciples, to make them as equipped and readied for their own challenges that would face them. They didn't understand completely, but the disciples trusted their lives to Jesus. Look, men, you're either all in or all out. You can't be lukewarm! To be a disciple (warrior) requires all of your focus and all of you. **Luke 14:27, 33** (NKJV) says, *"And whoever does not bear his cross and come after Me cannot be My disciple… So likewise, whoever of you does not forsake all that he has cannot be My disciple* [warrior]."

To be "perfectly trained" takes time. Jesus spent three full years developing the original twelve disciples. Modern day United States Army soldiers go through an extensive training program. First, they go to Basic Training that is divided into two parts: **Basic Combat Training** (BCT) and **Advanced Individual Training** (AIT). BCT consists of the first ten weeks of the total Basic Training period. AIT consists of the remainder of the total Basic Training period and is where recruits train in the specifics of their chosen field. As such, AIT is different for each available Army career path or Military Occupational Specialty (MOS). AIT courses can last anywhere from 4 to 52 weeks. Soldiers are still continually tested for physical fitness and weapons proficiency and are subject to the same duties, strict daily schedule, and disciplinary rules as in BCT. After graduation, soldiers will be assigned to their first duty location. Their training won't stop. They will continue learning how to apply their MOS to specific scenarios, all designed to broaden the soldier's capacity to fight and defeat any potential adversary or enemy to the United States of America. Throughout the soldiers' career, they will always be training and developing and will be given greater responsibilities, all designed to defeat the enemy.

As a warrior of God, you too have to be trained and equipped. Understand the enemy. Learn how to fight with the weapons given to you to defeat the enemies of our faith. You are expected to stand up against any harm that you, your family, your community, your country, and the "Body of Christ" may face. The weapons of your warfare are mighty and are able to decisively defeat the enemy.

Remember the nature of warfare. The enemy wants to defeat and destroy you. There is never a "fair fight." You either must completely destroy the enemy, or he will completely destroy you. Watch out! Jesus said in **John 10:10**, *"The thief does not come except to steal, and to kill, and to destroy. I have come that they may have life, and that they may have it more abundantly."*

During my deployment to Afghanistan in 2013, while on Forward Operation Base (FOB) Gamberi in Laghman Province, the entire FOB was placed on heightened security. An intelligence report stated that a local national worker was going to attempt to come onto the FOB wearing a suicide vest with the purpose of killing as many Americans as possible. The FOB was already operating in a high state of security and readiness. Perimeter walls with razor wire on top surrounded the FOB, and the wall had manned guard towers. Vehicles entering or exiting the FOB went through double check points, which used mirrors to check the underside of each vehicle. Guards carried live ammunition in their weapons in the event that they had to engage an enemy at a moment's notice. Every soldier on the FOB had to be within an arm's length of his protective body armor. But during this heightened security period, every soldier had to wear his full body armor everywhere they went on the FOB. Additional vehicle checks were made, where every passenger had to get out of the vehicle and the vehicle was thoroughly checked inside and out. Every pedestrian walking on to the FOB went through additional security checks. The threat was taken very seriously; lives were at stake. After three day of operating in this posture, the individual was caught without incident or harm to any soldier.

Who is your enemy? Sometimes you can't identify all of them. They are often disguised and undetected. But make no mistake, you are being watched for weaknesses and points of vulnerability so these weaknesses can be exploited.

Let's continue on with our study and equip ourselves as warriors and men after God's own heart.

Recognizing the Fight and Equipping the Warrior

Read Ephesians 6:10-18 (MEV)

Finally, my brothers, be strong in the Lord and in the power of His might.

[11]Put on the whole armor of God that you may be able to stand against the schemes of the devil.

[12]For our fight is not against flesh and blood, but against principalities, against powers, against the rulers of the darkness of this world, and against spiritual forces of evil in the heavenly places.

[13]Therefore take up the whole armor of God that you may be able to resist in the evil day, and having done all, to stand.

[14]Stand therefore, having your waist girded with truth, having put on the breastplate of righteousness,

[15]having your feet fitted with the readiness of the gospel of peace,

[16]and above all, taking the shield of faith, with which you will be able to extinguish all the fiery arrows of the evil one.

[17]Take the helmet of salvation and the sword of the Spirit, which is the word of God.

[18]Pray in the Spirit always with all kinds of prayer and supplication. To that end be alert with all perseverance and supplication for all the saints.

DISCUSSION

From where or whom does your strength come? Who puts on the armor? You or someone else? Why put it on in the first place? Against whom or what are you fighting? What does it mean to you that we wrestle not against flesh and blood? Can you describe the different types of enemies we face? What part of your armor should you use when attacked? Describe the different parts of your armor: truth, the breastplate of righteousness, your feet fitted with readiness and peace, the shield of faith, the helmet of salvation, and the sword of the Spirit. What part does prayer play in our fight against the enemy?

Study Notes

_____

_____

_____

_____

_____

Character Traits of the Warrior

Read 1 Peter 5:8-11 (MEV)

Be sober and watchful, because your adversary the devil walks around as a roaring lion, seeking whom he may devour.

⁹Resist him firmly in the faith, knowing that the same afflictions are experienced by your brotherhood throughout the world.

¹⁰But after you have suffered a little while, the God of all grace, who has called us to His eternal glory through Christ Jesus, will restore, support, strengthen, and establish you.

¹¹To Him be glory and dominion forever and ever. Amen.

DISCUSSION

What does the enemy want to do to your faith and life? How should you ready yourself to resist your enemy? What traits and qualities can you pull out of this passage that you can use in your fight with the adversary? Is there a purpose for your testing?

Army Values

Many people know what the words loyalty, duty, respect, selfless service, honor, integrity, and personal courage mean. But how often do you see someone actually live up to them? Soldiers learn these values in detail during Basic Combat Training (BCT); from then on, they live them every day in everything they do—whether they're on or off the job. In short, the seven core Army values listed below are what being a soldier is all about. How does this look for the Christian man who is daily walking out his commitment to Christ?

Loyalty

Bear true faith and allegiance to the US Constitution, the Army, your unit, and other soldiers. Bearing true faith and allegiance is a matter of believing in and devoting yourself to something or someone. A loyal soldier is one who supports the leadership and stands up for fellow soldiers. By wearing the uniform of the US Army, you are expressing your loyalty. And by doing your share, you show your loyalty to your unit.

Encouragement: As a Christian warrior, I will faithfully commit to the Lordship of Jesus Christ in my life and give myself completely to the body of Christ and other Christians. I will build up, encourage, and pray for my leadership. I will lend a hand to a fellow believer. I will be dependable and trustworthy to my local body of Christ.

Duty

Fulfill your obligations. Doing your duty means more than carrying out your assigned tasks. Duty means being able to accomplish tasks as part of a team. The work of the US Army is a complex combination of missions, tasks, and responsibilities—all in constant motion. Their work entails building one assignment onto another. Soldiers fulfill their obligations as a part of their unit every time they resist the temptation to take "shortcuts" that might undermine the integrity of the team.

Encouragement: As a Christian warrior, I will fulfill any and all commitments made. I won't allow others to pull my weight or responsibilities. I will do my part in the body of Christ. In all that I do, I will not damage the image of the Christian.

Respect

Treat people as they should be treated. In the Soldier's Code, soldiers pledge to "treat others with dignity and respect while expecting others to do the same." Respect is what allows us to appreciate the best in other people. Respect is trusting that all people have done their jobs and fulfilled their duty. Self-respect is a vital ingredient within the Army value of respect, which results from knowing you have put forth your best effort. The Army is one team, and each member has something to contribute.

Encouragement: As a Christian warrior, I will treat others as Jesus would treat them. I will esteem and value all people, regardless of their race, religion, gender, or ethnicity. I will seek never to disrespect others.

Selfless Service

Selfless service puts the welfare of the nation, the Army, and your subordinates before your own. Selfless service is larger than just one person. In serving your country, you are doing your duty loyally without thought of recognition or gain. The basic building block of selfless service is the commitment of each team member to go a little further, endure a little longer, and look a little closer to see how he or she can add to the effort.

Encouragement: As a Christian warrior, I will defer to the welfare of others before my own. I will attempt never to promote myself, but in all things lift up the strong name of Jesus and honor Him in all that I do. I will make every effort to give of myself completely to the body of Christ.

Honor

Live up to Army values. The nation's highest military award is the Medal of Honor and often given to soldiers who give the ultimate sacrifice, their lives, for the safety and wellbeing of others on their team. This award goes to soldiers who make honor a matter of daily living—soldiers who develop the habit of being honorable and solidify that habit with every value choice they make. Honor is a matter of carrying out, acting, and living the values of respect, duty, loyalty, selfless service, integrity, and personal courage in everything you do.

Encouragement: As a Christian warrior, I will daily live by the Word of God, applying it to every decision before me. With God's help, I will live a moral and principled life. I will daily seek to reflect Christ and, if required, lay down my life for Him.

Integrity

Do what's right legally and morally. Integrity is a quality you develop by adhering to moral principles. It requires that you do and say nothing that deceives others. As your integrity grows, so does the trust others place in you. The more choices you make based on integrity, the more this highly prized value will affect your relationships with family and friends and, finally, the fundamental acceptance of yourself.

Encouragement: As a Christian warrior, I will never intentionally violate the law, compromise my integrity, or bring shame upon Jesus Christ or the body of Christ. I will carefully carry the trust others place in me.

Personal Courage

Personal courage will enable you to face fear, danger, or adversity (physical or moral). Personal courage has long been associated with the Army. Physical courage is a matter of enduring physical duress and at times risking personal safety. Facing moral fear or adversity may be a long, slow process of continuing forward on the right path, especially if taking those actions is not popular with others. You can build your personal courage by daily standing up for and acting upon the things that you know are honorable

Encouragement: As a Christian warrior, I will not run away from any challenge placed before me because I know that I have on the complete armor of God and because the mighty hand of God is my defender. I am more than a conqueror in Christ Jesus. I will not knowingly or intentionally place myself in a morally compromising position. I will make decisions that honor Christ Jesus, even if others are not making the same decision.

Study Notes

_____

_____

_____

_____

_____

Read 2 Corinthians 10:3-6 (MEV)

For though we walk in the flesh, we do not war according to the flesh.

⁴For the weapons of our warfare are not carnal, but mighty through God to the pulling down of strongholds,

⁵casting down imaginations and every high thing that exalts itself against the knowledge of God, bringing every thought into captivity to the obedience of Christ,

⁶and being ready to punish all disobedience when your obedience is complete.

DISCUSSION

What does it mean that we don't walk or live in the flesh? Explain a stronghold? How do you pull down a stronghold? What would you say that your weapons can do for you? What must you do in order to be effective against your enemies and their strongholds? What and who are you warring against? Where is your battleground? Is there a world that you cannot see with your natural eye? If so, what and who exists there? What are your instruments for combat? How are you supposed to fight your battles?

Study Notes

_____

_____

_____

_____

_____

Application: Sun Tzu, the sixth century BC Chinese general, military strategist, and author of *The Art of War*, said the following:

> All warfare is based on deception. If you know your enemy and you know yourself, you need not fear the results of a hundred battles. If you know yourself but not the enemy, for every victory gained you will also suffer a defeat. If you know neither the enemy nor yourself, you will succumb in every battle. To know your enemy, you must become your enemy. What is of supreme importance in war is to attack the enemy's strategy. He who knows when he can fight and when he cannot will be victorious.

Men, your enemy wants to completely destroy you! Don't miscalculate, misjudge, or mistake the seriousness of the threat. All around you, the forces of evil are engaged in a battle for dominion over your life and the lives of others. We need to stand up and be vigilant, alert, and on guard. Always be ready. Know your weapons with which you have been equipped. Learn to be an expert in fighting with them. Lean not to your own understanding. We are on the winning team, and the forces of Satan lose! They are powerless against the forces of God.

The armor of God equips the warrior for battle. No warrior would ever go in to any kind of battle untrained and without the full complement of protective armor. Understand your enemy and his strengths and weaknesses. Firmly stand, established and protected against daily trials and temptations. Gird yourself. Prepare yourself for the conflicts that you may face by wrapping yourself in truth. The belt of truth lays a foundation. Truth always prevails over deception and over the schemes made in the dark places surrounding your life. Truth combats error and wrong thinking. Truth connects to the other parts of the armor. What is truth? God is truth. There is no lie within Him.

God is the rock upon which we build our lives. Stand fast on the firm foundation of righteousness. Who is righteous? Jesus is the embodiment of righteousness. Being in right standing before God comes through Jesus Christ. Put on the breastplate of righteousness. Put on the righteousness of Jesus and apply it to all areas of your life.

Shod your feet with the gospel of peace. Take on peace in your life. Don't be anxious for anything. Completely rest in the confidence that the Lord is your defender and your rear guard. Cover yourself with the shield of faith. The shield covers your entire body so there is no exposed part that the Enemy can attack. Protect your mind, will, and emotions by wearing the helmet of salvation. You have been transformed into a new man, and the salvation you received when you surrendered your life to the Lordship of Jesus Christ completely recreated your life and opened you up to the plans and purposes God had for your life. Your salvation brought you out of a life of broken relationship with God to a right relationship with God.

Finally, daily fight every confrontation with the sword of the Spirit, the truth and assurance found in the Word of God. The sword of the Spirit crushes every deception, scheme, and harassment from the enemy. When you have completely put on all of your armor, pray. Pray without ceasing, in all that you do. Keep in the constant fellowship with God that is found in prayer. The Holy Spirit helps us to pray. He knows the heart of the Father and the Son. He intercedes for you before, during, and after a conflict.

The warrior must always be on guard and aware that the enemy is lurking and waiting to come against him. Daily you should be watchful, sober-minded, clear-thinking, alert, diligent, and cautious at all times. Be aware that your enemy wants to completely ruin your faith and life. He draws us through lies and temptations, coupled with our own inclination to be selfish. If we believe a lie and act on it, then we reap the consequences of the associated choices we make. We might not have intended to cause harm, but damage was the result.

A sentry or a guard who was caught sleeping on his post was often put to death because of his lack of responsibility to protect from potential danger. Others depended on his vigilance. You too stand to be put to death, either physically or spiritually, when you are not vigilant to stand guard against our Enemy, Satan, as he seeks to destroy you and others under your care.

———

Personal Story: The military has the custom of exchanging a hand salute when a junior soldier passes a senior officer. The salute is not a subservient act or gesture but quite the contrary. According to FM 7-21.13 in *The Soldier's Guide:*

> The salute is an expression that recognizes each other as a member of the profession of arms; that they have made a personal commitment of self-sacrifice to preserve our way of life. The fact that the junior extends the greeting first is merely a point of etiquette—a salute extended or returned makes the same statement.

During the salute, often courtesies are exchanged, such as "Good morning, Sir" or "Good evening, Ma'am" or maybe a unit motto.

While I was serving with the 504th Battlefield Surveillance Brigade out of Fort Hood, Texas, from August 2013 to January 2015, the unit deployed to Kosovo in 2014. In the 504th during the exchange of hand salutes, the soldier initiating the salute and greeting would say, "Always Ready," and the response from the senior would be "Vigilance." Since being in the unit, I have thought about and enjoyed that greeting and exchange. As a Christian, I have given it a great deal of thought and reflection as it pertains to our daily walk before others and God. Every day, in every circumstance, we should be vigilant and always ready. We should be ready to give an answer for the hope that lies within us, ready to share how our lives have changed because of how God transformed our lives. We should be vigilant and always ready to face the daily attacks to our faith that come from influences all around us. As in the military, we have to train and equip ourselves.

Faithfully take in the Word of God, pray, and fellowship with other Christians as you walk out your faith. I salute you, my reader, and say "Always Ready," to which I hope you will reply, "Vigilance."

The 504th Battlefield Surveillance Brigade is the "Always Ready Brigade." You can be the "Always Ready Christian"!

Every day you are marching into a battle of spiritual warfare. The implication is similar to a military combat soldier going into a war zone. So you too are in a spiritual battle that competes for your existence, pulling at the very fabric of your life. Jesus faced the Prince of this World, Lucifer or Satan, in the desert. You must face daily the enemies that have aligned themselves with Satan, wrestling for your life and pulling at your heart to submit and join them. Each day has enough challenges to test and try you, but remember that Jesus triumphed over our Enemy and empowers you to be victorious too! You are empowered by the Holy Spirit in the same way as Jesus when He faced His conflicts. You can destroy the assaults against you. Be strong in the power of the Lord. He is your defender. Even though you have to live in your earthly body, you do not have to be controlled by its nature. Instead you can yield to the influence of God's nature. Be encouraged, my brother. You are on the winning side and are not alone. Be strong in the power and strength of the Lord.

Further Study

Joshua 23:10	1 Kings 2:2	2 Chronicles 15:7
Psalm 18:29, 89:14	Isaiah 40:31	Zechariah 4:6
Romans 13:12	1 Corinthians 16:13	1 Thessalonians 5:8
1 Timothy 1:18, 19; 6:11-16	2 Timothy 2:3-5	Hebrews 10:32
James 4:7	1 John 4:4; 5:5	Revelation 2:22; 12:17

Notes

_____

_____

_____

_____

_____

_____

_____

_____

_____

"The LORD is a warrior..."
Exodus 15:3 (NET)

Part 2: The Warrior Ring

Lesson 6
Daily Surrender on the Altar

WHEN I WAS stationed in Germany in the Army, my day typically started around 4:30 in the morning. After shaving, I would drive to the post for morning accountability and physical training, which would last from 1 to 1.5 hours, and then drive back home. Then after personal hygiene, I would return to the base for a normal 8- to 10-hour workday. During that time, my duties would range from training meetings to circulation through the motor pool to check on the equipment status for both field artillery weapon systems and supporting wheeled vehicles. Then I sometimes needed to follow up on any small arms that were in a stage of repair. Then I would check on the welfare of the soldiers in the unit. Slowly circulating through the battery, I would talk to each of the soldiers so I could make a determination on their welfare. If there was a concern, it would be brought up to their chain of command.

Next was the training for the day. Was it being followed? Were the training objectives being met? Did everyone show up for the training? Throughout the day, unknowns would pop up. I would have to solve problems and confront them with the NCO's (non-commissioned officers) and other officers in the unit. Decisions would have to be made to solve the issues. Now this was the schedule for a typical day, one when we were not alerted at 3:00 in the morning.

When we were alerted, we would have to come into the unit, load up all of our equipment, and be ready to cross the departure point by a certain time. Once the departure point was crossed, we would then move to our predetermined assembly or rally points. This exercise might last from two to four hours. Once the exercise was complete, we would recover our equipment, vehicles, and personnel back to the unit's motor pool. After recovery, the normal day would begin.

The purpose of the exercises was to ensure that the unit was in a constant state of readiness. A daily preparedness was always being assessed. There was a known enemy against whom we continuously readied ourselves. If our mental, physical, and tactical skills were not entirely focused on our daily requirements, soldiers could have been hurt—or worse.

We too, as Christian men, have to be prepared. We must daily choose to surrender ourselves to the mission (the will of God) that God places before us. If we don't prepare ourselves mentally, physically, or most importantly spiritually for the potential fight facing us, we could be hurt or lose ground to the spiritual Enemy who lurks, waiting to attack. You can't start your daily preparation at midday; you must start at the beginning of your day. It's essential to make a daily commitment to the Lord. You may not have a physical formation that you show up for each day, but you still need to show up each day. The body of Christ is depending on you to be in a ready state, prepared for your assignment. **Proverbs 3:5-8** (MEV) says, *"Trust in the LORD with all your heart, and lean not on your own understanding; ⁶in all your ways acknowledge Him, and He will direct your paths. ⁷Do not be wise in your own eyes; fear the LORD and depart from evil. ⁸It will be health to your body, and strength to your bones."*

Psalm 118:24 (MEV) says, *"This is the day that the LORD has made; we will rejoice and be glad in it."* Wake up each day and commit everything to the Lord! Brothers, we are in this fight together. Daily surrender yourself to all that the Lord has for you. He can be trusted, and others are trusting you to be ready too.

DISCUSSION

This is the day the Lord has made. How should you greet your day? Why? How much of your heart should you trust to the Lord? Is your understanding enough?

Study Notes

_____

_____

_____

_____

_____

Daily Present Yourself

Read Galatians 2:20 (AMP)

I have been crucified with Christ [in Him I have shared His crucifixion]; it is no longer I who live, but Christ (the Messiah) lives in me; and the life I now live in the body I live by faith in (by adherence to and reliance on and complete trust in) the Son of God, Who loved me and gave Himself up for me.

Read 1 Corinthians 15:31, 36 (NKJV)

I affirm, by the boasting in you which I have in Christ Jesus our Lord, I die daily.

[36]Foolish one, what you sow is not made alive unless it dies.

Read Romans 12:1, 2 (MEV)

I urge you therefore, brothers, by the mercies of God, that you present your bodies as a living sacrifice, holy, and acceptable to God, which is your reasonable service of worship.

[2]Do not be conformed to this world, but be transformed by the renewing of your mind, that you may prove what is the good and acceptable and perfect will of God.

DISCUSSION

What are these verses telling us about how we should approach each new day of our lives? What does it mean to you to present yourself as a "living sacrifice"? What does it mean to live by faith? How does faith apply to your daily decisions? How are you tempted to conform to this world?

Study Notes

Daily Conflict

Read Matthew 11:29, 30 (NKJV)

Take My yoke upon you and learn from Me, for I am gentle and lowly in heart, and you will find rest for your souls.

[30]For My yoke is easy and My burden is light."

Read 2 Corinthians 4:16-18 (NKJV)

Therefore we do not lose heart. Even though our outward man is perishing, yet the inward man is being renewed day by day.

[17]For our light affliction, which is but for a moment, is working for us a far more exceeding and eternal weight of glory,

[18]while we do not look at the things which are seen, but at the things which are not seen. For the things which are seen are temporary, but the things which are not seen are eternal.

Read Psalm 55:22 (AMP)

Cast your burden on the Lord [releasing the weight of it] and He will sustain you; He will never allow the [consistently] righteous to be moved (made to slip, fall, or fail).

Read 1 John 5:5 (TLB)

But who could possibly fight and win this battle except by believing that Jesus is truly the Son of God?

DISCUSSION

What is a yoke? What yoke do you think God wants to put on you? What does the Bible say about Jesus' yoke? Why should we not lose heart? Do you think it is reasonable to expect to have affliction in your life? Would it be unrealistic to hope to avoid all affliction? How should you look at or embrace affliction in your life? Should you carry your burdens on your own or in your own strength? Can you fight your battles on your own? Why not?

Study Notes

_____

_____

_____

_____

_____

Daily Walk

Read 1 Kings 2:3 (AMP)

Keep the charge of the Lord your God, walk in His ways, keep His statutes, His commandments, His precepts, and His testimonies, as it is written in the Law of Moses, that you may do wisely and prosper in all that you do and wherever you turn.

Read Isaiah 43:2 (NASB)

When you pass through the waters, I will be with you; And through the rivers, they will not over-flow you. When you walk through the fire, you will not be scorched, Nor will the flame burn you.

Read Psalm 25:9 (NKJV)

The humble He guides in justice, And the humble He teaches His way.

Read Colossians 2:20-23 (TLB)

Since you died, as it were, with Christ and this has set you free from following the world's ideas of how to be saved—by doing good and obeying various rules —why do you keep right on following them anyway, still bound by such rules as

²¹not eating, tasting, or even touching certain foods?

²²Such rules are mere human teachings, for food was made to be eaten and used up.

²³These rules may seem good, for rules of this kind require strong devotion and are humiliating and hard on the body, but they have no effect when it comes to conquering a person's evil thoughts and desires. They only make him proud.

Read Hebrews 13:15, 16 (MEV)

Through Him, then, let us continually offer to God the sacrifice of praise, which is the fruit of our lips, giving thanks to His name.

¹⁶But do not forget to do good and to share. For with such sacrifices God is well pleased.

DISCUSSION

How should you daily walk? What are the benefits of keeping God's commandments, His statutes, and His precepts? Will you be harmed as a result of going through the daily trials of your life? Why not? What assurance do you have? Describe what being humble means to you? How much do you want to be taught by God? How has Christ set you free from following worldly ideas? Which ones have you gained victory over in your daily walk? What is praise to you? How can you offer a daily sacrifice of praise to God?

Study Notes

_____

_____

_____

_____

_____

Daily Expectation

Read Luke 12:35-40 (NKJV)

"Let your waist be girded and your lamps burning;

³⁶and you yourselves be like men who wait for their master, when he will return from the wedding, that when he comes and knocks they may open to him immediately.

³⁷Blessed are those servants whom the master, when he comes, will find watching. Assuredly, I say to you that he will gird himself and have them sit down to eat, and will come and serve them.

³⁸And if he should come in the second watch, or come in the third watch, and find them so, blessed are those servants.

³⁹But know this, that if the master of the house had known what hour the thief would come, he would have watched and not allowed his house to be broken into.

⁴⁰Therefore you also be ready, for the Son of Man is coming at an hour you do not expect."

Read Matthew 25:1-12 (MEV)

"Then the kingdom of heaven shall be like ten virgins, who took their lamps and went out to meet the bridegroom.

²Five of them were wise and five were foolish.

³Those who were foolish took their lamps, but took no oil with them.

⁴But the wise took jars of oil with their lamps.

⁵While the bridegroom delayed, they all rested and slept.

⁶But at midnight there was a cry, 'Look, the bridegroom is coming! Come out to meet him!'

⁷Then all those virgins rose and trimmed their lamps.

⁸But the foolish said to the wise, 'Give us some of your oil, for our lamps have gone out.'

⁹The wise answered, 'No, lest there not be enough for us and you. Go rather to those who sell it, and buy some for yourselves.'

¹⁰"But while they went to buy some, the bridegroom came, and those who were ready went in with him to the wedding banquet. And the door was shut.

¹¹Afterward, the other virgins came also, saying, 'Lord, Lord, open the door for us.'

¹²But he answered, 'Truly I say to you, I do not know you.'"

DISCUSSION

These two verses are talking about the same thing: being ready. How should you live daily so you can be ready for the Lord's return? What does it mean to you to be "found watching"? Why is a thief mentioned in the passage? What is the nature of a thief? Describe the difference between the "wise" and the "foolish" virgins. Have you ever fallen asleep, lost focus, or drifted while waiting for the Lord?

Study Notes

_____

_____

_____

_____

_____

Daily Practices

Read 1 Thessalonians 4:3-8 (MEV)

For this is the will of God, your sanctification: that you should abstain from sexual immorality,
⁴that each one of you should know how to possess his own vessel in sanctification and honor,
⁵not in the lust of depravity, even as the Gentiles who do not know God,
⁶and that no man take advantage of and defraud his brother in any matter, because the Lord is the avenger in all these things, as we also have forewarned you and testified.
⁷For God has not called us to uncleanness, but to holiness.
⁸Therefore he that despises does not despise man, but God, who has also given us His Holy Spirit.

Read Psalm 119:1-3 (MEV)

Blessed are those whose way is blameless, who walk in the law of the LORD.
²Blessed are those who keep His testimonies, and who seek Him with all their heart.
³They also do no wrong; they walk in His ways.

Read Job 31:1 (MEV)

"I made a covenant with my eyes; why then should I look upon a young woman?

Read Psalm 101:3 (MEV)

I will set no wicked thing before my eyes.

Read Proverbs 13:20 (MEV)

He who walks with wise men will be wise, but a companion of fools will be destroyed.

Read 1 Thessalonians 5:17, 18 (MEV)

Pray without ceasing.
¹⁸In everything give thanks, for this is the will of God in Christ Jesus concerning you.

DISCUSSION

What does sanctification mean to you? What does abstain mean? How do you daily apply abstaining to your life? In your own words, describe "possess your own vessel" and "lust of depravity." Is holiness an out-of-date or old-fashioned idea for today? Why or why not? This verse says it's possible "to do no wrong." What do you think about that? Does it matter what you daily look at? Should you be accountable for what you see? What detractors cause your eyes to wander? How can you protect your mind? Do the people you daily choose to hang out with matter in your growth or in your sensitivity to listening to the Holy Spirit? How so? Why should you daily read and take in the Word of God? How often should you pray? How does prayer strengthen your daily walk (relationship) with God?

Study Notes

_____

_____

_____

_____

_____

Read Proverbs 27:19 (NKJV)

As in water face reflects face, So a man's heart reveals the man.

DISCUSSION

Only you truly know what is in your heart. Others may not, but God can clearly see what you think is hidden. Take a moment to reflect and listen. Is there a need for any change? Is there any need for you to lay that thought, deed, or action on the altar before God?

Study Notes

_____

_____

_____

_____

_____

Application: **Romans 12:1** (AMPC) says, *"I APPEAL to you therefore, brethren, and beg of you in view of [all] the mercies of God, to make a decisive dedication of your bodies [presenting all your members and faculties] as a living sacrifice, holy (devoted, consecrated) and well pleasing to God, which is your reasonable (rational, intelligent) service and spiritual worship."*

Throughout Scripture, the altar was connected with a significant encounter with God. It marked that point in time where a life changed, where there was a sacrifice on the part of an individual. That sacrifice was demonstrated with an offering that cost something. Then every time the individual passed that altar, it served as a reminder of the covenantal relationship of trust between the individual and God. The relationship cost the individual something, but God was also committed to the relationship.

The altar serves as a visual symbol and reminder of being in the center of God's will—the daily living out of a desire to be in the center of God's will. A sacrificial covenant can be made at any juncture of your life. The result of the encounter is a greater heart's devotion toward God, to one's vocation (calling), to one's spouse or family, or to those entrusted to your care. The altar nowadays can serve as a reminder to daily stay faithful, pure (in thought, attitude, and action), and true to that decision made before God to fulfill your life's purpose.

James 1:22-25 (MEV) says, *"Be doers of the word and not hearers only, deceiving yourselves. 23For if anyone is a hearer of the word and not a doer, he is like a man viewing his natural face in a mirror. 24He views himself, and goes his way, and immediately forgets what kind of man he was. 25But whoever looks into the perfect law of liberty, and continues in it, and is not a forgetful hearer but a doer of the work, this man will be blessed in his deeds."*

Even though we don't physically build altars to God anymore, we can still make daily sacrifices before God. You can make a daily sacrifice of praise and thanksgiving. You can pray and intercede for others, your family, your city, and your nation. You can sacrifice your time. What part of your life should be laid down before God and sacrificed? Be honest and transparent. Is there a place where your relationship has gone astray? Your relationship can be set straight and started fresh. Once that part of your life is laid on the altar and your sin is repented of, God remembers it no more. Understand that God is supreme—beneath nothing—so why focus on lesser things? You need to be committed with all your heart. You can't have a divided heart. Chose this day whom you will serve: the one true, living God or a dead, lifeless substitute. Paul said in **Acts 26:29** (AMPC), *"...I would to God that not only you, but also all who are listening to me today, might become such as I am, except for these chains."* The words *"become such as I am"* indicate a desire for your life to reflect Jesus so much, without saying a word, that others would want to become like you.

It's not until you give and sacrifice of yourself completely that you discover who you are. We say

WWJD (What Would Jesus Do), but in order to find a place of understanding, we must become less so He can become greater within our lives. We gain nothing by being self-centered but gain everything by being others-focused. How hard is it to encourage or say thank you? Let others know you appreciate them and what they have done. Daily lay down on the altar yourself so you can truly find out who you were meant to be. Imitate the goodness of God in your life; become a mirror that reflects Him to others. In all your ways, acknowledge Him. We are His lights. Daily make the choice to surrender.

The Enemy works very hard to distract you from reading your Bible, listening to inspirational music, praying, fellowshipping with others in the body of Christ, and having a relationship with the Holy Spirit because all of these life choices will revolutionize your life and make you more like Jesus. They are like Miracle-Gro for your spiritual life. The more you feed on them, the faster you will grow spiritually.

1 Samuel 16:7 (NKJV) says, *"But the LORD said to Samuel, 'Do not look at his appearance or at his physical stature, because I have refused him.* **For the LORD does not see as man sees; for man looks at the outward appearance, but the LORD looks at the heart'** *"* (Boldness added). Daily surrender and reflect all of Jesus through your life.

The Warrior Creed

The Word of God is the standard and inspiration for my life;
I believe every word it says;
I believe what it says about me;
I will daily live by the Word of God as the Holy Spirit of God lives in and through me;
I am a man after God's own heart.

© Evan Trinkle

Further Study

Proverbs 27:19	Jeremiah 31:31-34	Hosea 10:2
Matthew 6:22, 23, 31-33	Matthew 10:38; 16:24	Luke 9:23, 24, 59; 14:27, 33
Romans 6:6	2 Corinthians 3:14-18	Galatians 6:14
Colossians 2:20; 3:3	Hebrews 7:22-28; 10:16, 17	James 1:22-25
1 John 2:3-17		

Notes

Conclusion

Wow! YOU MADE IT! You are in the twelfth round of the spiritual boxing heavyweight championship of the world. You're drained of all of your energy, and you don't know if you have the strength to finish the last round. You're mentally challenged, and you've been running on adrenaline for the last three rounds. Your coach in the corner is yelling at you, trying to get your attention so he can tell you to hang in there. This is the last round. Reach deep inside of yourself to find the strength to face your opponent for just three more minutes. You have to keep your guard up. If you drop your guard, your opponent can get in a jab or even a knockout punch. If you make it through the round, you will win the bout!

Throughout this study, it has been emphasized that your choices matter. Choosing to complete the study mattered. You have been challenged and stretched, and growth has taken place in your life. You are not alone. Your brothers to the left and right of you have been right there with you. You have shared common experiences and grown to trust each other. You have deepened friendships and trust among brothers in the Lord. All of you are in the trenches together, alongside of each other. You have not been on your journey alone, nor will you be as you continue to daily walk out your life.

Ecclesiastes 4:9, 10, 12 (NKJV) says, *"Two are better than one, Because they have a good reward for their labor. ¹⁰For if they fall, one will lift up his companion. But woe to him who is alone when he falls, For he has no one to help him up. ¹²Though one may be overpowered by another, two can withstand him. And a threefold cord is not quickly broken."*

I would say to you, "Who do you say Jesus is?" Make your choice, but you can only be in one camp—not two. You can't straddle the fence. You either deny yourself, take up your cross, and follow Jesus, or you deny Jesus and live your own life without the mercy and grace of God over your life. Choose carefully and remember—what good is it if you should gain the whole world yet forfeit your soul?

Remember what is at stake!

Luke 9:23-27 (NKJV) says, *"Then He said to them all, 'If anyone desires to come after Me, let him deny himself, and take up his cross daily, and follow Me. ²⁴For whoever desires to save his life will lose it, but whoever loses his life for My sake will save it. ²⁵For what profit is it to a man if he* *gains the whole world, and is himself destroyed or lost? ²⁶For whoever is ashamed of Me and My words, of him the Son of Man will be ashamed when He comes in His own glory, and in His Father's, and of the holy angels. ²⁷But I tell you truly, there are some standing here who shall not taste death till they see the Kingdom of God."*

So now the challenge is before you: what is your next decision? Again you have come to a fork in the road with many choices. Your resolution will prove itself out. Before you is the same choice Joshua had: "Choose you this day whom you will serve" (**Joshua 24:15**). As we have seen throughout this study, it's about your choices. When you choose, remember the following words: "If God is for you, who can be against you."

> "Sow a thought and you reap an action;
> sow an act and you reap a habit;
> sow a habit and you reap a character;
> sow a character and you reap a destiny."
> – Ralph Waldo Emerson

One definition of *destiny*: "The things that you will do, or the type of person that you will become, in the future."

Galatians 6:7-10 (NKJV) says, *"Do not be deceived, God is not mocked; for whatever a man sows, that he will also reap. ⁸For he who sows to his flesh will of the flesh reap corruption, but he who sows to the Spirit will of the Spirit reap everlasting life. ⁹And let us not grow weary while doing good, for in due season we shall reap if we do not lose heart. ¹⁰Therefore, as we have opportunity, let us do good to all, especially to those who are of the household of faith."*

You sow and you reap. You have control of that process because you freely choose. Every man can become better. Like a plant, if you expose yourself to the right light and plenty of water, you will grow. There will be no change in your life without a daily commitment to apply what you have learned in this study. Remember God, others, family, and self; think of Jesus on the cross, think of the tomb, think of the Holy Spirit, and think of the fruit of the Spirit; don't forget daily vigilance, the armor of God, and daily surrender on the altar each and every day. You will have up days and down days; that is the cycle of growth. Fellowship with God in His Word and with other believers, either in church or small group settings, will strengthen you. *"As iron sharpens iron, so one man sharpens another"* (**Proverbs 27:17**, NIV). You are not alone. Enjoy your life and remember that you are a child of AlmightyGod, created in His image and designed to have fellowship with Him and to reflect His precious Holy Spirit through your daily life. God never leaves you; He is always walking by your side.

Ecclesiastes 3:1 (NKJV) says, *"To everything there is a season, A time for every purpose under heaven."* Commit to applying the life principles learned in this study, review them, and meditate on them. As they soak into your spirit, they will become a part of who you are and what defines you as a man. It is no mistake that you have studied these lessons and come to this place in your life. Let the Word of God guide you. Proverbs 3:5-7 (NKJV) says, *"Trust in the LORD with all your heart, And lean not on your own understanding;* ⁶*In all your ways acknowledge Him, And He shall direct your paths.* ⁷*Do not be wise in your own eyes; Fear the LORD and depart from evil."*

The plans and purposes God has for you are between you and Him. He equips and strengthens you to fulfill what He has called you to do. The Holy Spirit helps you daily in the process. We all need to develop character, which enables us to mirror the Lord in our lives.

The Word of God says in Isaiah 26:3 (NKJV) *"You [God] will keep him in perfect peace, Whose mind is stayed on You, Because he trusts in You."* My friend, rest and completely trust in the One Who is trustworthy. Be anxious for nothing, but every day learn to let go of how you think your life should look. Instead, let God bring your life to you. Our God is an awesome God. Amen!

Colossians 2:6-10 (MEV) says, *"As you have received Christ Jesus the Lord, so walk in Him,* ⁷*rooted and built up in Him and established in the faith, as you have been taught, and abounding with thanksgiving.* ⁸*Beware lest anyone captivate you through philosophy and vain deceit, in the tradition of men and the elementary principles of the world, and not after Christ.*

⁹*For in Him lives all the fullness of the Godhead bodily.* ¹⁰*And you are complete in Him, who is the head of all authority and power."*

The power of God gives us the strength to live. The Holy Spirit enables us. We represent Jesus. The only Jesus others may see is the example they see in us as it is lived out before them.

This journey of life that you are on will have many doors. This study you have just completed is one of them. Each door will enrich, encourage, and strengthen you. Surround yourself with people who will help you grow; expose yourself to materials that challenge you and add to your development as a man of God, a man after God's heart. Never be satisfied with where you are now. Press in and constantly ask the Holy Spirit to inspire and open up to you His wisdom, understanding, and truth. Allow Him to guide you and to speak into your life daily over every choice you're facing—no matter how great or small.

David was approximately 16 years old when he was anointed by Samuel to be God's choice as the next king of Israel. It's not your age that God looks at, but your heart. Do you have a heart that seeks God? Develop a passion to put God first in your life. Allow Him to open up doors in your life that no person can shut and to close any doors that would prevent benefit in your life. Trust God completely. Will you do that?

I love you, my brother. Now share what you have learned with another. Start your own small group and show others where Give away freely what insight God has given you. As you give, you receive. It's the "law of reciprocity." You can't out give God. Lean on the Holy Spirit. Place yourself in situations where you need the Holy Spirit to show up and help you. You are promised His help, and you are not alone. Be a man after God's own heart.

Write to the following email and tell us how this study has impacted your life so we can share and encourage others through your testimony: acovenantheart@gmail.com

Appendix 1
Additional Suggestions for Small Groups Leaders

THANK YOU AGAIN FOR having a heart for men and men's ministry. It is very pleasing to God that you are standing in your role as leader and facilitator of your group. A part of being a leader is also learning to listen. When your group is in session, listen. Listen to the responses given by each man during times of sharing. Listen for re-occurring concerns and needs. Listen for what the Holy Spirit is saying to you during that time. Ask the Holy Spirit to help you blend together the responses and concerns given by the men in the group with the topic and theme from the study and what He is guiding you to say to the group.

Participation is invaluable. As you get to know each man's personality in the group, you will have a feel for where he is in his walk with the Lord. Draw each man into participation in the group. As iron sharpens iron, so one man will sharpen the other. We learn from each other. Just be sensitive not to push too hard because you may push a man away from the group.

TIME MANAGEMENT OF THE CLASS

You may have from one hour to one and a half hours for your meeting. Each lesson is packed with potential topics and will foster much group discussion. Balance the time for discussion with the goal of completing the lesson each week. Be aware of the direction that the Holy Spirit is taking the group's discussion. Have a heart for spontaneity if needed. Watch yourself so that you are not too rigid and time-structured, so that you create an environment where men feel they can't share their thoughts and impressions. Foster an environment where all of the men develop a heart for one another.

Another valuable commitment is to take the time to call each man in your group at least once a week. Spend about 5 to 15 minutes with him. Ask him how his week is going. Ask if there is anything in the study he particularly enjoys. Does he have any needs for which you can pray? Then if possible, pray together before ending the call. Genuinely care and again listen. Others will share if they know you care for them. Take time to get to know the men in your group. During a phone call or personal one-on-one talk, if you learn of any special needs or struggles that a man may have, ask him for permission to bring it up to the whole group or encourage him to bring it up for group prayer. Men bond together when there is a shared need or an area they can contribute toward solving.

When you pray for each man in the group, keep a prayer journal. Watch how God moves in the group. Write down when and how God answers the prayer requests. Be encouraged by the hand of God and encourage others as He moves in your group.

Have fun. Enjoy leading the group. Grow with the group. God will stretch you too. Embrace every opportunity to lean on the Holy Spirit for guidance, wisdom, and discernment. Allow yourself to be a vessel that God can flow through to minister to the needs of other men.

Each time the group gathers, the Holy Spirit will be there too. The dynamics of each meeting will be special for that meeting. Never be overly concerned with who is or who is not at the group. When there is ministry going on, the Lord is there. You can minister to one or all of the group. Don't qualify what the Lord wants to do through you.

If you need a coach or mentor to lean on, ask your pastor for assistance. You are always welcome to reach out to the author of this study by email at acovenantheart@gmail.com.

Thank you for walking this journey. I'm excited for you and grateful that you have a heart for men's ministry.

Through Christ,

Your Brother

Appendix 2
Suggestions for the Covenant Signing

A. The Covenant Signing

THE SIGNING SHOULD BE led by the group leader. The "Warrior Covenant" can be signed either in the place where the study is taking place or before the church body. What each man has gone through to this point in his journey should be emphasized and reviewed. Remind them to keep their eyes on what lies ahead and all that they will study in the future. Discuss what they will learn and grow into as iron sharpens iron. Their commitment to be transformed by the Holy Spirit will grow. It takes a special man to have a commitment to follow God's plan for his life. Focus to keep eternity as your prize and to set daily priorities. Like a band of brothers, these men are a part of God's plan for fellowship together in their goal to be a man after God's own heart.

Appendix 3
Suggestions for a Ring Ceremony

IRST, DECIDE IF THE pastor or the study group leader is going to officiate the ceremony. If the pastor is going to officiate, then the group leader will support. It is our suggestion that if the group is connected to a local church body, the pastor should officiate the ceremony. The ceremony and presentation of a ring may be celebrated before the church body or the study group. Family and friends gather to honor the commitment to be a man after God's own heart.

The Ring Ceremony

Officiate:

Wow! These men have made it! They are now in the twelfth round of the spiritual boxing heavyweight championship of the world. They are drained of energy and don't know if they have the strength to finish the last round. They have been mentally challenged and running on adrenaline for the last three rounds. Their coach, God Himself, is in the corner yelling, trying to get their attention so he can tell them to hang in there. He says, "This is the last round. Reach deep inside of yourself to find the strength to face your opponent for just three more minutes. Keep your guard up. If you drop your guard, your opponent can get in a jab or even a knockout punch. If you make it through the round, you will win the bout!"

Standing before you this day are God's modern-day warriors, fighting for and living by the Word of God.

Throughout this study, it has been emphasized that choices matter. Choosing to complete this study mattered. These men have been challenged and stretched, and growth has taken place in their lives. They have not been alone. Their brothers to the left and right have been right there with them. They have shared common experiences and grown to trust each other. Friendship and trust among brothers in the Lord have deepened. They have been in the trenches together, alongside of each other. They have not been on this journey alone, nor will they be as they continue to daily walk out their life's journey.

Ecclesiastes 4:9, 10, 12 (NKJV) says, *"Two are better than one, Because they have a good reward for their labor. ¹⁰For if they fall, one will lift up his companion. But woe to him who is alone when he falls, For he has no one to help him up. ¹²Though one may be overpowered by another, two can withstand him. And a threefold cord is not quickly broken."*

Luke 9:23-27 (NKJV) says, *"Then He said to them all, 'If anyone desires to come after Me, let him deny himself, and take up his cross daily, and follow Me. ²⁴For whoever desires to save his life will lose it, but whoever loses his life for My sake will save it. ²⁵For what profit is it to a man if he gains the whole world, and is himself destroyed or lost? ²⁶For whoever is ashamed of Me and My words, of him the Son of Man will be ashamed when He comes in His own glory, and in His Father's, and of the holy angels. ²⁷But I tell you truly, there are some standing here who shall not taste death till they see the kingdom of God.' "*

Every man standing before you has become better. The journey they have been on consisted of a two-part study. Part one began with the "Warrior Covenant," where they looked at their covenant with God, Family, Others, and Self. Then they signed what is call the "Warrior Covenant." Then in part two, they studied the elements of the "Warrior Ring," which they are receiving today. Those elements consisted of Jesus on the cross, the tomb, the Holy Spirit, the fruit of the Spirit, daily vigilance, the armor of God, and finally daily surrender on the altar each and every day. Proverbs says, *"As iron sharpens iron, so one man sharpens the other"* (27:17). These men have sharpened each other, encouraged each other, and at times held the other up.

God is continuing to reveal the plans and purposes for each of these men. He is equipping and strengthening them to fulfill what He has called them to do. The Holy Spirit is helping them daily in that process.

Colossians 2:6-9 (MEV) says, *"As you have received Christ Jesus the Lord, so walk in Him, ⁷rooted and built up in Him and established in the faith, as you have been taught, and abounding with thanksgiving. ⁸Beware lest anyone captivate you through philosophy and vain deceit, in the tradition of men and the elementary principles of the world, and not after Christ. ⁹For in Him lives all the fullness of the Godhead bodily. ¹⁰And you are complete in Him, who is the head of all authority and power."*

It is the power of God that gives us the strength to live. The Holy Spirit enables us. We represent Jesus. The only Jesus others may see is the example they see in us as it is lived out before them.

This journey these men now face will have many doors. This study they have recently completed is just one of them. Gentlemen, my brothers, commit to being a man after God's heart.

Remember, David was most likely only 16 years old when he was anointed by Samuel to be God's choice as the next king of Israel. It's not your age that God looks at but your heart. Have a heart that seeks God. Develop a passion to put God first in your life. Allow Him to open doors in your life that no person can shut or to close doors that would prevent benefits to your life. Trust God completely. Will you do that?

Finally, be a man after God's own heart.

Call each man's name and present him his ring.

A Special Note

To make the ceremony more of a special event, announce it in your church bulletin if you have one. Have a photographer available and invite family members.

Announce the time of the next men's class so that those men who did not make it to this class can attend the next one.

Finally, send pictures of your ceremony to acovenantheart@gmail.com so they can be shared with the greater community of men seeking to be a man after God's own heart.

Acknowledgments

"The Lord is a warrior..."
Exodus 15:3 (NET)

I WOULD LIKE TO EXTEND a special thanks to Chaplains Mark Hart and Thomas "Tom" Gorrell. Without their encouragement, this study would never have been launched. They pushed me when I wanted to procrastinate or set the study to the side. I appreciate you, Tom and Mark.

Thanks to Pastor Steve Pearson, senior pastor of Church of the Savior in Lexington, Kentucky, who was interested in the study and gave positive feedback. Steve's contribution of "adultery warnings" was both insightful and significant in its impact on the message of this study.

Also, thank you to Christopher Robertson, who was bold enough to give me the first honest feedback while the study was in its beginning phases.

In addition, I would like to give a special thank you to Steve Strang, Founder/CEO of Charisma Media. Steve has coached, encouraged, and gently but firmly pushed me through the writing of this study. I have never written a book before, and Steve helped me through the highs and lows of the journey. He has been a wonderful mentor and guide, for which I am very grateful.

Then I would also like to thank the many men who participated in pilot studies. Your feedback provided invaluable input in shaping how the study material would be presented.

Special appreciation is extended to pastors Ken Groen, Stephen Blandino, Jeremy White, and Eddie Mallonee. In addition, Greg Williams and Mike Wallace, thank you very much for your help in making this study come together.

I would like to extend my appreciation to Rena Fish, who edited, proofread and put the finishing touches on my manuscript, and to Linda Stubblefield, who managed to brilliantly format the study.

Made in United States
Orlando, FL
13 May 2025

61211883R00118